Growing in the Gospel

The Psalms Project Volume Eight

Discovering the Spiritual World through the Psalms – Psalm 71-80

Michael Harvey Koplitz

All Scripture quotations, unless otherwise noted, are taken from the New American Standard Bible®, Copyright © 1960, 1962, 1963, 1968, 1971, 1972, 1973, 1975, 1977, 1995 by the Lockman Foundation. Used by permission (www.Lockman.org)

The NASB uses italic to indicate words that have been added for clarification. Citations are shown with large capital letters.

TABLE OF CONTENTS

The goal of this project:

This research project will examine the 150 psalms for the spiritual awareness each Psalm offers. Each Psalm will be examined by its language and the commentary of the Sages. The spiritual awareness analysis will be done in alignment with Ari's definition of the Tree of life, the Book of Creation, and the Zohar. Each verse of the Psalm will be rewritten using the intent of the language and spiritual commentary to convey its spiritual lesson.

The main resources:

The Zohar

The Book of Creation

Ari's writing on the Tree of Life and the Ten Sefirot

The Theological Wordbook of the Old Testament

Samson Hirsch's commentary on the Psalms

Tehillim – Psalms – A new translation with a commentary anthologized from the Talmudic and rabbinic sources

Accordance Bible Software

Psalm 71

New American Standard 1995	Hebrew
Psa. 71:1 *a*In You, O LORD, I have taken refuge; Let me never be ashamed. 2 *a*In Your righteousness deliver me and rescue me; *b*Incline Your ear to me and save me. 3 *a*Be to me a rock of *b*habitation to which I may continually come; You have given *c*commandment to save me, For You are *d*my [1]rock and my fortress. 4 *a*Rescue me, O my God, out of the hand of the wicked, Out of the [1]grasp of the wrongdoer and ruthless man, 5 For You are my *a*hope; O Lord [1]GOD, *You are* my *b*confidence from my youth. 6 [1]By You I have been *a*sustained from *my* birth; You are He who *b*took me from my mother's womb; My *c*praise is continually [2]of You. **Psa. 71:7** I have become a *a*marvel to many, For You are *b*my strong refuge. 8 My *a*mouth is filled with Your praise And with *b*Your glory all day long. 9 Do not cast me off in the *a*time of old age; Do not forsake me when my strength fails.	בְּךָֽ־יְהוָ֥ה חָסִ֑יתִי **Psa. 71:1** אַל־אֵב֥וֹשָׁה לְעוֹלָֽם׃ 2 בְּצִדְקָתְךָ֥ תַּצִּילֵ֗נִי וּֽתְפַלְּטֵ֑נִי הַטֵּֽה־אֵלַ֥י אָ֝זְנְךָ֗ וְהוֹשִׁיעֵֽנִי׃ 3 הֱיֵ֤ה לִ֨י ׀ לְצ֥וּר מָע֡וֹן לָב֗וֹא תָּמִ֗יד צִוִּ֥יתָ לְהוֹשִׁיעֵ֑נִי כִּֽי־ סַלְעִ֖י וּמְצוּדָתִ֣י אָֽתָּה׃ 4 אֱֽלֹהַ֗י פַּ֭לְּטֵנִי מִיַּ֣ד רָשָׁ֑ע מִכַּ֖ף מְעַוֵּ֣ל וְחוֹמֵֽץ׃ 5 כִּֽי־ אַתָּ֥ה תִקְוָתִ֑י אֲדֹנָ֥י יְהוִ֝֗ה מִבְטַחִ֥י מִנְּעוּרָֽי׃ 6 עָלֶ֤יךָ ׀ נִסְמַ֨כְתִּי מִבֶּ֗טֶן מִמְּעֵ֣י אִמִּ֣י אַתָּ֣ה גוֹזִ֑י בְּךָ֖ תְהִלָּתִ֣י תָמִֽיד׃ 7 כְּ֭מוֹפֵת הָיִ֣יתִי לְרַבִּ֑ים וְ֝אַתָּ֗ה מַֽחֲסִי־עֹֽז׃ 8 יִמָּ֣לֵא פִ֭י תְּהִלָּתֶ֑ךָ כָּל־הַ֝יּ֗וֹם תִּפְאַרְתֶּֽךָ׃ 9 אַֽל־תַּ֭שְׁלִיכֵנִי לְעֵ֣ת זִקְנָ֑ה כִּכְל֥וֹת כֹּ֝חִ֗י אַֽל־ תַּֽעַזְבֵֽנִי׃ 10 כִּֽי־אָמְר֣וּ אוֹיְבַ֣י לִ֑י וְשֹׁמְרֵ֥י נַ֝פְשִׁ֗י נוֹעֲצ֥וּ

10   For my enemies have spoken ¹against me;

And those who ᵃwatch for my ²life ᵇhave consulted together,

11   Saying, "ᵃGod has forsaken him;

Pursue and seize him, for there is ᵇno one to deliver."

Psa. 71:12   O God, ᵃdo not be far from me;

O my God, ᵇhasten to my help!

13   Let those who are adversaries of my soul be ᵃashamed *and* consumed;

Let them be ᵇcovered with reproach and dishonor, who ᶜseek ¹to injure me.

14   But as for me, I will ᵃhope continually,

And will ¹ᵇpraise You yet more and more.

15   My ᵃmouth shall tell of Your righteousness

And of ᵇYour salvation all day long;

For I ᶜdo not know the ¹sum *of them.*

16   I will come ᵃwith the mighty deeds of the Lord ¹GOD;

I will ᵇmake mention of Your righteousness, Yours alone.

Psa. 71:17   O God, You ᵃhave taught me from my youth,

And I still ᵇdeclare Your wondrous deeds.

18   And even when *I am* ᵃold and gray, O God, do not forsake me,

Until I ᵇdeclare Your ¹strength to *this* generation,

Your power to all who are to come.

יַחְדָּו ׃ לֵאמֹר אֱלֹהִים עֲזָבוֹ 11
רְדְפוּ וְתִפְשׂוּהוּ כִּי־אֵין
מַצִּיל ׃ אֱלֹהִים אַל־תִּרְחַק 12
מִמֶּנִּי אֱלֹהַי לְעֶזְרָתִי חִישָׁה
[חוּשָׁה ׃] יֵבֹשׁוּ יִכְלוּ שֹׂטְנֵי 13
נַפְשִׁי יַעֲטוּ חֶרְפָּה וּכְלִמָּה
מְבַקְשֵׁי רָעָתִי ׃ וַאֲנִי תָּמִיד 14
אֲיַחֵל וְהוֹסַפְתִּי עַל־כָּל־
תְּהִלָּתֶךָ ׃ פִּי ׀ יְסַפֵּר 15
צִדְקָתֶךָ כָּל־הַיּוֹם תְּשׁוּעָתֶךָ
כִּי לֹא יָדַעְתִּי סְפֹרוֹת ׃ 16
אָבוֹא בִּגְבֻרוֹת אֲדֹנָי יְהוִה
אַזְכִּיר צִדְקָתְךָ לְבַדֶּךָ ׃ 17
אֱלֹהִים לִמַּדְתַּנִי מִנְּעוּרָי
וְעַד־הֵנָּה אַגִּיד נִפְלְאוֹתֶיךָ ׃
וְגַם עַד־זִקְנָה ׀ וְשֵׂיבָה 18
אֱלֹהִים אַל־תַּעַזְבֵנִי עַד־
אַגִּיד זְרוֹעֲךָ לְדוֹר לְכָל־
יָבוֹא גְּבוּרָתֶךָ ׃ וְצִדְקָתְךָ 19
אֱלֹהִים עַד־מָרוֹם אֲשֶׁר־
עָשִׂיתָ גְדֹלוֹת אֱלֹהִים מִי
כָמוֹךָ ׃ אֲשֶׁר הִרְאִיתַנוּ 20
[הִרְאִיתַנִי ׀] צָרוֹת רַבּוֹת

19 ¹For Your *a*righteousness, O God, *reaches* to the ²heavens,

You who have *b*done great things;

O God, *c*who is like You?

20 You who have *a*shown ¹me many troubles and distresses

Will *b*revive ¹me again,

And will bring ¹me up again *c*from the depths of the earth.

21 May You increase my *a*greatness

And turn *to* *b*comfort me.

Psa. 71:22 I will also praise You with ¹*a*a harp,

Even Your ²truth, O my God;

To You I will sing praises with the *b*lyre,

O *c*Holy One of Israel.

23 My lips will *a*shout for joy when I sing praises to You;

And my *b*soul, which You have redeemed.

24 My *a*tongue also will utter Your righteousness all day long;

For they are *b*ashamed, for they are humiliated who seek ¹my hurt.

וְּרֹעוֹת תָּשׁוּב תְּחַיֵּינוּ
[תְּחַיֵּינִי] וּמִתְּהֹמוֹת הָאָרֶץ
תָּשׁוּב תַּעֲלֵנִי: 21 תֶּרֶב |
גְּדֻלָּתִי וְתִסֹּב תְּנַחֲמֵנִי: 22
גַּם־אֲנִי | אוֹדְךָ בִכְלִי־נֶבֶל
אֲמִתְּךָ אֱלֹהַי אֲזַמְּרָה לְךָ
בְכִנּוֹר קְדוֹשׁ יִשְׂרָאֵל: 23
תְּרַנֵּנָּה שְׂפָתַי כִּי אֲזַמְּרָה־
לָּךְ וְנַפְשִׁי אֲשֶׁר פָּדִיתָ: 24
גַּם־לְשׁוֹנִי כָּל־הַיּוֹם תֶּהְגֶּה
צִדְקָתֶךָ כִּי־בֹשׁוּ כִי־חָפְרוּ
מְבַקְשֵׁי רָעָתִי:

References

Psalm 71:1
[a]Ps 25:2, 3; 31:1-3; 71:1-3

Psalm 71:2
[a]Ps 31:1
[b]Ps 17:6

Psalm 71:3
[1]Or *crag*
[a]Ps 31:2, 3
[b]Deut 33:27; Ps 90:1; 91:9
[c]Ps 7:6; 42:8
[d]Ps 18:2

Psalm 71:4
[1]Lit *palm*
[a]Ps 140:1, 4

Psalm 71:5
[1]Heb *YHWH,* usually rendered *LORD*
[a]Ps 39:7; Jer 14:8; 17:7, 13, 17; 50:7
[b]Ps 22:9

Psalm 71:6
[1]Lit *Upon You I have been supported*
[2]Lit *in*
[a]Ps 22:10; Is 46:3
[b]Job 10:18; Ps 22:9
[c]Ps 34:1

Psalm 71:7
[a]Is 8:18; 1 Cor 4:9
[b]Ps 61:3

Psalm 71:8
[a]Ps 35:28; 63:5
[b]Ps 96:6; 104:1

Psalm 71:9
[a]Ps 71:18; 92:14; Is 46:4

Psalm 71:10
[1]Lit *with reference to*
[2]Lit *soul*
[a]Ps 56:6
[b]Ps 31:13; 83:3; Matt 27:1

Psalm 71:11
[a]Ps 3:2
[b]Ps 7:2

Psalm 71:12
[a]Ps 10:1; 22:11; 35:22; 38:21
[b]Ps 38:22; 40:13; 70:1, 5

Psalm 71:13
[1]Lit *my injury*
[a]Ps 35:4, 26; 40:14
[b]Ps 109:29
[c]Esth 9:2; Ps 71:24

Psalm 71:14
[1]Lit *add upon all Your praise*
[a]Ps 130:7
[b]Ps 71:8

Psalm 71:15
[1]Lit *numbers*
[a]Ps 35:28
[b]Ps 96:2
[c]Ps 40:5

Psalm 71:16
[1]Heb *YHWH,* usually rendered *LORD*
[a]Ps 106:2
[b]Ps 51:14

Psalm 71:17
[a]Deut 4:5; 6:7

[b]Ps 26:7; 40:5; 119:27

Psalm 71:18
[1]Lit *arm*
[a]Ps 71:9
[b]Ps 22:31; 78:4, 6

Psalm 71:19
[1]Or *And*
[2]Lit *height*
[a]Ps 36:6; 57:10
[b]Ps 126:2; Luke 1:49
[c]Deut 3:24; Ps 35:10

Psalm 71:20
[1]Another reading is *us*
[a]Ps 60:3
[b]Ps 80:18; 85:6; 119:25; 138:7; Hos 6:1, 2
[c]Ps 86:13

Psalm 71:21
[a]Ps 18:35
[b]Ps 23:4; 86:17; Is 12:1; 49:13

Psalm 71:22
[1]Lit *an instrument of a harp*
[2]Or *faithfulness*
[a]Ps 33:2; 81:2; 92:1-3; 144:9
[b]Ps 33:2; 147:7
[c]2 Kin 19:22; Ps 78:41; 89:18; Is 1:4

Psalm 71:23
[a]Ps 5:11; 32:11; 132:9, 16
[b]Ps 34:22; 55:18; 103:4

Psalm 71:24
[1]Or *to injure me*
[a]Ps 35:28
[b]Ps 71:13

Targum

Psa. 71:1 In your word, O LORD, I have put my trust; I will never be disappointed. **2** In your generosity deliver me and save me; incline your ear to me and redeem me. **3** Be a strong mighty rock for me always to come to; you have given commandment to redeem me, for you are my strength and my stout fortress. **4** O God, save me from the hand of the wicked man, from the hand of the wrongdoer and the predator. **5** For you are my hope, O LORD; my God, my confidence from my youth. **6** I have relied on you from the womb; you bring me out of the bowels of my mother; my Psalm is always of your word. **7** I have became like a portent for many; and you are my confidence and my strength. **8** My mouth will be filled with your praise, with your splendor every day. **9** Do not cast me away at the time of old age; when my vigor ceases, do not forsake me. **10** For my enemies have spoken evil about me, and those who watch my soul have conspired together. **11** Saying, "God has forsaken him; pursue and catch him, for there is no one to deliver [him]." **12** O God, do not be far from me; O my God, hasten to my aid. **13** Let those who oppose my soul be disappointed [and] destroyed; let those who seek my ruin be covered with disgrace and dishonor. **14** And I will always wait, and I will add to all your praise. **15** My mouth will tell of your generosity, of your redemption every day, for I do not know their number. **16** I will enter in the strength of the LORD God; I will remember your righteousness alone. **17** O my God, you have taught me by miracles from my youth; and to this very time I will tell of your marvels. **18** And moreover, O God, do not forsake me at the time of old age and gray hair, until I may tell of the strength of your arm to every generation, of your mighty strength to all who will come. **19** Your righteousness, O God, [reaches] to the highest heaven, for you have done great things; O God, who is like you? **20** You who have shown me great and evil troubles, make us live again; and bring us up again from the deepest depths. **21** You will increase my greatness, and you will turn and comfort me. **22** Also I will give thanks in your presence with instruments of song, and the lyre; I will tell of your truth, O my God, I will sing praise in your presence with the harp, Holy One of Israel. **23** My lips will rejoice, for I will give praise in your presence, and [also] my soul that you have redeemed. **24** Also my tongue every day will repeat your generosity, for those who seek my ruin have been disappointed, they have been put to shame. –

Spiritual Awareness

Due to the length of the Psalm, only the spiritual awareness of verses will be explored.

Introduction

This Psalm is a continuation of Psalm 70. David was near his death and feared he might not live to regain his royal throne. He, therefore, pleaded with God to rejuvenate him. Absolom, David's son, had started a rebellion against his father. At one point during the rebellion, Absolom conquered Jerusalem. He was ready to declare himself King. David fled from Jerusalem before Absolom could capture him. Eventually, David did stop the rebellion. At the writing of this Psalm, David was concerned that he would not be able to regain the throne. He wanted to live up to what the LORD wanted him to do. The rebellion occurred because of David's immoral affair with Bathsheba.

Verse two

David knew that, eventually, the LORD would deliver him from the rebellion. He pleaded with the LORD to allow him to escape the rebellion's destruction. David prayed to deliver him back to the throne.

In Your merciful justice You will deliver me and You will let me escape; now incline Your ear to me and save me.

Verse five

There is a balance between justice and mercy in the LORD's Universe. The Sefirot Gevurah and Chesed are the top of two of the three columns in the Tree of Life. How can mercy be shown when justice is needed?

For You have been my hope; my Master, Who shows mercy from the Sefirah Chesed even as the Seforah Gevurah is giving out justice. You have had my trust from my youth.

Verse six

David did not have a happy childhood. He was the youngest of eight sons and not well-treated by his older brothers. His father misunderstood him and made him a shepherd over the flocks. When Samuel came to Jesse's house to find the next King of Israel, David was almost overlooked. David found little love and understanding from his nuclear family, forcing him to look to his inner resources for comfort.

On You I relied for support from birth; You have set me apart from my mother's womb; from You it would always come about whatever was to be praise worthy in me.

Verses twelve and thirteen

The gravity of David's sin was quite enormous. However, David asked the LORD to remain close to him even now as the Sefirah Gevurah passes judgment.

O God, be not far from me; O my God, make haste to help me.

Verse Fifteen

David did not understand how the Tree of Life worked. Therefore, he did not know how Chesed and Gevurah went hand in hand.

My mouth shall tell of Your merciful justice, and of your Salvation every day, for I have never know how to emmeraete them.

Verse nineteen

The power of the ten Sefirot radiate from Heaven into all areas of the Universe.

For Your merciful justice reaches into high heavens, O You who have done great things, O God, who is like you?

Psalm 72

New American Standard 1995	Hebrew
Psa. 72:0 *A Psalm* of Solomon.	
Psa. 72:1 Give the King [a]Your judgments, O God, And [b]Your righteousness to the King's son. 2 [1]May [2]he [a]judge Your people with righteousness And [3b]Your afflicted with justice. 3 [1]Let the mountains bring [2a]peace to the people, And the hills, in righteousness. 4 [1]May he [a]vindicate the [2]afflicted of the people, Save the children of the needy And crush the oppressor.	לִשְׁלֹמֹה ׀ אֱלֹהִים **Psa. 72:1** מִשְׁפָּטֶיךָ לְמֶלֶךְ תֵּן וְצִדְקָתְךָ לְבֶן־מֶלֶךְ ׃ 2 יָדִין עַמְּךָ בְצֶדֶק וַעֲנִיֶּיךָ בְמִשְׁפָּט ׃ 3 יִשְׂאוּ הָרִים שָׁלוֹם לָעָם וּגְבָעוֹת בִּצְדָקָה ׃ 4 יִשְׁפֹּט ׀ עֲנִיֵּי־עָם יוֹשִׁיעַ לִבְנֵי אֶבְיוֹן וִידַכֵּא עוֹשֵׁק ׃ 5 יִירָאוּךָ עִם־ שֶׁמֶשׁ וְלִפְנֵי יָרֵחַ דּוֹר
Psa. 72:5 [1]Let them fear You [a]while the sun *endures,* And [2]as long as the moon, throughout all generations. 6 [1]May he come down [a]like rain upon the mown grass, Like [b]showers that water the earth. 7 In his days [1]may the [a]righteous flourish, And [b]abundance of peace till the moon is no more.	דּוֹרִים ׃ 6 יֵרֵד כְּמָטָר עַל־גֵּז כִּרְבִיבִים זַרְזִיף אָרֶץ ׃ 7 יִפְרַח־בְּיָמָיו צַדִּיק וְרֹב שָׁלוֹם עַד־בְּלִי יָרֵחַ ׃ 8 וְיֵרְדְּ מִיָּם עַד־יָם וּמִנָּהָר עַד־
Psa. 72:8 May he also rule [a]from sea to sea And from the River to the ends of the earth. 9 [1]Let [a]the nomads of the desert [b]bow before him, And his enemies [c]lick the dust.	אַפְסֵי־אָרֶץ ׃ 9 לְפָנָיו יִכְרְעוּ צִיִּים וְאֹיְבָיו עָפָר יְלַחֵכוּ ׃ 10 מַלְכֵי תַרְשִׁישׁ וְאִיִּים מִנְחָה יָשִׁיבוּ מַלְכֵי שְׁבָא וּסְבָא אֶשְׁכָּר יַקְרִיבוּ ׃ 11 וְיִשְׁתַּחֲווּ־

10 ¹Let the kings of ᵃTarshish and of the ²ᵇislands bring presents;
The kings of ᶜSheba and ᵈSeba ᵉoffer ³gifts.
11 ¹And let all ᵃkings bow down before him,
All ᵇnations serve him.

Psa. 72:12 For he will ᵃdeliver the needy when he cries for help,
The ¹afflicted also, and him who has no helper.
13 He will have ᵃcompassion on the poor and needy,
And the ¹lives of the needy he will save.
14 He will ¹ᵃrescue their ²life from oppression and violence,
And their blood will be ᵇprecious in his sight;
15 So may he live, and may the ᵃgold of Sheba be given to him;
And let ¹them pray for him continually;
Let ¹them bless him all day long.

Psa. 72:16 May there be abundance of grain in the earth on top of the mountains;
Its fruit will wave like *the cedars of* ᵃLebanon;
And may those from the city flourish like ᵇvegetation of the earth.
17 May his ᵃname endure forever;
May his name ¹increase ²ᵇas long as the sun *shines;*
And let *men* ᶜbless themselves by him;
ᵈLet all nations call him blessed.

לוֹ כָל־מְלָכִים כָּל־גּוֹיִם
יַעַבְדוּהוּ ׃ 12 כִּי־יַצִּיל אֶבְיוֹן
מְשַׁוֵּעַ וְעָנִי וְאֵין־עֹזֵר לוֹ ׃ 13
יָחֹס עַל־דַּל וְאֶבְיוֹן וְנַפְשׁוֹת
אֶבְיוֹנִים יוֹשִׁיעַ ׃ 14 מִתּוֹךְ
וּמֵחָמָס יִגְאַל נַפְשָׁם וְיֵיקַר
דָּמָם בְּעֵינָיו ׃ 15 וִיחִי וְיִתֶּן־לוֹ
מִזְּהַב שְׁבָא וְיִתְפַּלֵּל בַּעֲדוֹ
תָמִיד כָּל־הַיּוֹם יְבָרֲכֶנְהוּ ׃ 16
יְהִי פִסַּת־בַּר ׀ בָּאָרֶץ בְּרֹאשׁ
הָרִים יִרְעַשׁ כַּלְּבָנוֹן פִּרְיוֹ
וְיָצִיצוּ מֵעִיר כְּעֵשֶׂב הָאָרֶץ ׃
17 יְהִי שְׁמוֹ לְעוֹלָם לִפְנֵי־
שֶׁמֶשׁ יָנִין [יִנּוֹן] שְׁמוֹ
וְיִתְבָּרְכוּ בוֹ כָּל־גּוֹיִם
יְאַשְּׁרוּהוּ ׃ 18 בָּרוּךְ ׀ יְהוָה
אֱלֹהִים אֱלֹהֵי יִשְׂרָאֵל עֹשֵׂה
נִפְלָאוֹת לְבַדּוֹ ׃ 19 וּבָרוּךְ ׀
שֵׁם כְּבוֹדוֹ לְעוֹלָם וְיִמָּלֵא
כְבוֹדוֹ אֶת־כָּל־הָאָרֶץ אָמֵן
וְאָמֵן ׃ 20 כָּלּוּ תְפִלּוֹת דָּוִד
בֶּן־יִשָׁי ׃

<table>
<tr><td>

Psa. 72:18 Blessed be the LORD God, the God of Israel,

    Who alone works wonders.

19   And blessed be His glorious name forever;

    And may the whole earth be filled with His glory.

    Amen, and Amen.

Psa. 72:20   The prayers of David the son of Jesse are ended.

</td><td></td></tr>
</table>

References

Psalm 72:1
[a]1 Kin 3:9; 1 Chr 22:13
[b]Ps 24:5

Psalm 72:2
[1]Or *He* will judge
[2]Many of the pronouns in this Psalm may be rendered *He* since the typical reference is to the Messiah
[3]Or *Your humble*
[a]Is 9:7; 11:2-5; 32:1
[b]Ps 82:3

Psalm 72:3
[1]Or *The mountains will bring*
[2]Or *prosperity*
[a]Is 2:4; 9:5, 6; Mic 4:3, 4; Zech 9:10

Psalm 72:4
[1]Or *He will vindicate*
[2]Or *humble*
[a]Is 11:4

Psalm 72:5
[1]Or *They will fear*
[2]Lit *before the moon*
[a]Ps 72:17; 89:36, 37

Psalm 72:6
[1]Or *He will come down*
[a]Deut 32:2; 2 Sam 23:4; Hos 6:3
[b]Ps 65:10

Psalm 72:7
[1]Or *the righteous will flourish*
[a]Ps 92:12
[b]Is 2:4

Psalm 72:8

*[a]*Ex 23:31; Zech 9:10

Psalm 72:9

[1]Or *The nomads...will bow*
*[a]*Ps 74:14; Is 23:13
*[b]*Ps 22:29
*[c]*Is 49:23; Mic 7:17

Psalm 72:10

[1]Or *The kings...will bring*
[2]Or *coastlands*
[3]Or *tribute*
*[a]*2 Chr 9:21; Ps 48:7
*[b]*Ps 97:1; Is 42:4, 10; Zeph 2:11
*[c]*1 Kin 10:1; Job 6:19; Is 60:6
*[d]*Gen 10:7; Is 43:3
*[e]*Ps 45:12; 68:29

Psalm 72:11

[1]Or *All kings will bow down*
*[a]*Ps 138:4; Is 49:23
*[b]*Ps 86:9

Psalm 72:12

[1]Or *humble*
*[a]*Job 29:12; Ps 72:4

Psalm 72:13

[1]Lit *souls*
*[a]*Prov 19:17; 28:8

Psalm 72:14

[1]Lit *redeem*
[2]Lit *soul*
*[a]*Ps 69:18
*[b]*1 Sam 26:21; Ps 116:15

Psalm 72:15

[1]Lit *him*
*[a]*Is 60:6

Psalm 72:16
[a]Ps 104:16
[b]Job 5:25

Psalm 72:17
[1]Or *sprout forth*
[2]Lit *before the sun*
[a]Ex 3:15; Ps 135:13
[b]Ps 89:36
[c]Gen 12:3; 22:18
[d]Luke 1:48

Psalm 72:18
[a]1 Chr 29:10; Ps 41:13; 89:52; 106:48
[b]Ex 15:11; Job 5:9; Ps 77:14; 86:10; 136:4

Psalm 72:19
[a]Neh 9:5; Ps 96:8
[b]Num 14:21
[c]Ps 41:13

Targum

Psa. 72:1 Composed by Solomon, uttered in prophecy. O God, give your just rulings to the King Messiah, and your righteousness to the son of King David. **2** Let him judge your people in righteousness, and your poor with just rulings. **3** The inhabitants of the mountains will lift up peace for the house of Israel, and the hills in purity. **4** He will judge the poor of the people, he will redeem the sons of the lowly, and he will purge away the oppressor. **5** They will fear you at the rising of the sun, and they will pray in your presence before the light of the moon for all generations. **6** He will descend like the favorable rain on the grass that is cut because of locusts, like the drops of late rain that drip on the grass of the earth. **7** The righteous will increase in his days, and peace abound, until those who worship the moon are destroyed. **8** And he will rule from the bank of the Great Sea to the bank of the Great Sea, and from the Euphrates to the ends of the earth. **9** The governors will bow down before him, and his enemies will lick the dust. **10** The kings of Tarsus and the islands of the ocean sea will bring back tribute; the kings of Sheba and Seba will offer gifts. **11** And all kings will do homage to him; all the Gentiles will submit to him. **12** For he will deliver the lowly who seeks favor, and the poor who have no helper. **13** He will pity the indigent and lowly, and he will redeem the souls of the lowly. **14** From duress and from extortion he will redeem their souls, and their blood will be precious in his presence. **15** And he will live and give to him some of the gold that they brought to him from Sheba, and he will pray for him always; every day he will bless him. **16** Let there be the support of bread in the land on the top of the mountains; its fruit will quiver like Lebanon, and they will blossom from the city of Jerusalem like the grass of the earth. **17** May his name be invoked for ever; and before the sun came to be his name was determined; so all the peoples will be blessed by his merit, and they shall speak well of him. **18** Blessed is the LORD God, God of Israel, who works great wonders by himself. **19** And blessed is his glorious name forever, and let the whole earth be filled with his glorious splendor. Amen and amen. **20** The prayers of David son of Jesse are complete. --

Spiritual Awareness

Introduction

This Psalm is the last one of the Second book of Psalms. It is also the last Psalm dedicated to events in King David's life. The sage Radak said that David was near death when he wrote this Psalm. The day of its creation was a triumphant day of celebration. David had crowned Solomon to replace him as the King of Israel. There was an unprecedented celebration that day. As David reviewed the events of his life, he realized that many of his cherished plans for creating a perfect society based on the Torah remain unfulfilled. David charged Solomon to be his spiritual heir with creating a utopian world order predicated on Divine righteousness and justice.

Verse three

An additional task has been given to the LORD's people. The LORD himself sanctified this task, and that is

צַדִּיק "is used attributively when applied to God himself as to his character. The Lord is the just judge (2 Chr 12:6; Ps 11:7; Jer 12:1; Lam 1:18) even to the utmost degree as the judge of all the earth (Deut 32:4; Ps 119:137; Isa 5:16). Therefore his standards, his judgments set out in his word are righteous (Ps 119:144, 160, 172). Being everlasting, they are the confidence of his people and will not fall. God's hate of sin and love of righteousness (45:7 [H 8]) express his essential righteousness. Therefore righteousness and judgment are the habitation ("foundation" NASB, NIV) of God's throne, i.e. they always characterize his actions (97:2)."[1]

---

[1] The Wordbook of the Old Testament electronic verse from Accordance Bible software. 2023.

This factor will finally complete the state founded upon the LORD's Torah and enable faithful Shalom (peace). This factor is charity. A society based on the Torah needs to take care of one another. A conscientious sense of duty toward the LORD and voluntary service to one's brothers is necessary.

This verse is written metaphorically by David.

Metaphorical translation - But the mountains bring peace to the people and the hills through a sense of duty.

Spiritual translation – May the people have peace through their duty to the LORD and their brothers and sisters.

Verse six

In verse five, David said the people should revere the LORD before the King. The King and princes of the nation should come upon the people as rain from the sky. The word used for princes is the same term used for clouds. The idea is that the rain is a much-needed gift from the LORD. Israel was a land where water was always sparse. The King and Princes were to help the people to remain dedicated to the ways of the LORD and His Torah.

Metaphorical translation - May he descend like rain upon the mown meadow, as showers of rain, a waterer of the earth.

Spiritual translation – May the nation's King and princes help the people grow and prosper by following the ways of the Torah.

Verse seven

David hoped that Solomon and future kings would not be indiscriminate in their work on behalf of the people. The kings need to remember that they serve the people and not the other way around. The reference to the moon can be viewed as a desire to see that the reminders to the King and princes about their tasks will no longer be needed. The King and princes will instinctively know to take care of the people.

Metaphorical translation – May the righteous man flourish in his days, and the abundance of peace, until the moon shall be needed no more.

Spiritual translation – The righteous man shall flourish so opulently, and the welfare of all shall grow in such abundance that the awareness of God, shining through every body and soul, shall tolerate no darkness of night upon the earth, and the moon shall be needed no more.

Verse sixteen

When the King takes care of his people as his number one priority, the LORD will lavish the King and nation with material blessings. This is the reward for being the King that the LORD wants the King to be.

May the border of grain in the land extend upon the top of the mountains; may its fruit rustle like Lebanon, but as for them may they blossom out of the city like the grass of the earth.

Verse twenty

David will have completed his goal when all the blessings listed in the Psalm have been obtained.

Then the prayers of David, the son of Jessie, will be at an end.

Psalm 73

New American Standard 1995	Hebrew
Psa. 73:0 A Psalm of Asaph. **Psa. 73:1** Surely God is [a]good to Israel, To those who are [b]pure in heart! [2] But as for me, [a]my feet came close to stumbling, My steps [1]had almost slipped. [3] For I was [a]envious of the [1]arrogant *As* I saw the [b]prosperity of the wicked. [4] For there are no pains in their death, And their [1]body is fat. [5] They are [a]not [1]in trouble *as other* [2]men, Nor are they [b]plagued [3]like mankind. [6] Therefore pride is [a]their necklace; The [b]garment of violence covers them. [7] Their eye [1]bulges from [a]fatness; The imaginations of *their* heart [2]run riot. [8] They [a]mock and [1]wickedly speak of oppression; They [b]speak from on high. [9] They have [a]set their mouth [1]against the heavens, And their tongue [2]parades through the earth. **Psa. 73:10** Therefore [1]his people return to this place, And waters of [a]abundance are [2]drunk by them.	**Psa. 73:1** מִזְמֹ֗ור לְאָ֫סָ֥ף אַ֤ךְ טֹ֭וב לְיִשְׂרָאֵ֣ל אֱלֹהִ֑ים לְבָרֵ֥י לֵבָֽב׃ 2 וַאֲנִ֗י כִּ֭מְעַט נָטָ֣יוּ [נָטָ֑יוּ] רַגְלָ֑י כְּ֝אַ֗יִן שֻׁפְּכ֥ה [שֻׁפְּכ֥וּ] אֲשֻׁרָֽי׃ 3 כִּֽי־קִ֭נֵּאתִי בַּֽהֹולְלִ֑ים שְׁלֹ֖ום רְשָׁעִ֣ים אֶרְאֶֽה׃ 4 כִּ֤י אֵ֣ין חַרְצֻבֹּ֣ות לְמֹותָ֑ם וּבָרִ֥יא אוּלָֽם׃ 5 בַּעֲמַ֣ל אֱנֹ֣ושׁ אֵינֵ֑מֹו וְעִם־אָ֝דָ֗ם לֹ֣א יְנֻגָּֽעוּ׃ 6 לָ֭כֵן עֲנָקַ֣תְמֹו גַאֲוָ֑ה יַעֲטָף־שִׁ֝֗ית חָמָ֥ס לָֽמֹו׃ 7 יָ֭צָא מֵחֵ֣לֶב עֵינֵ֑מֹו עָ֝בְר֗וּ מַשְׂכִּיֹּ֥ות לֵבָֽב׃ 8 יָמִ֤יקוּ ׀ וִידַבְּר֣וּ בְרָ֣ע עֹ֑שֶׁק מִמָּרֹ֥ום יְדַבֵּֽרוּ׃ 9 שַׁתּ֣וּ בַשָּׁמַ֣יִם פִּיהֶ֑ם וּ֝לְשֹׁונָ֗ם תִּֽהֲלַ֥ךְ בָּאָֽרֶץ׃ 10 לָכֵ֤ן ׀ יָשִׁ֣יב [יָשׁ֣וּב] עַמֹּ֣ו הֲלֹ֑ם וּמֵ֥י מָ֝לֵ֗א יִמָּ֥צוּ לָֽמֹו׃ 11 וְֽאָמְר֗וּ אֵיכָ֥ה

11 They say, ""How does God know?
And is there knowledge [1]with the Most High?"
12 Behold, "these are the wicked;
And always "at ease, they have increased *in* wealth.
13 Surely "in vain I have [1]kept my heart pure
And "washed my hands in innocence;
14 For I have been stricken "all day long
And [1b]chastened every morning.

Psa. 73:15 If I had said, "I will speak thus,"
Behold, I would have betrayed the "generation of Your children.
16 When I "pondered to understand this,
It was [1]troublesome in my sight
17 Until I came into the [1a]sanctuary of God;
Then I perceived their "end.
18 Surely You set them in "slippery places;
You cast them down to [1b]destruction.
19 How they are [1a]destroyed in a moment!
They are utterly swept away by "sudden terrors!
20 Like a "dream when one awakes,
O Lord, when "aroused, You will "despise their [1]form.

Psa. 73:21 When my "heart was embittered
And I was "pierced [1]within,
22 Then I was "senseless and ignorant;
I was *like* [1]a "beast [2]before You.

יֵדַע־אֵל וְיֵשׁ דֵּעָה בְּעֶלְיוֹן׃	
12 הִנֵּה־אֵלֶּה רְשָׁעִים וְשַׁלְוֵי	
עוֹלָם הִשְׂגּוּ־חָיִל׃ **13** אַךְ־	
רִיק זִכִּיתִי לְבָבִי וָאֶרְחַץ	
בְּנִקָּיוֹן כַּפָּי׃ **14** וָאֱהִי נָגוּעַ	
כָּל־הַיּוֹם וְתוֹכַחְתִּי	
לַבְּקָרִים׃ **15** אִם־אָמַרְתִּי	
אֲסַפְּרָה כְמוֹ הִנֵּה דוֹר בָּנֶיךָ	
בָגָדְתִּי׃ **16** וָאֲחַשְּׁבָה לָדַעַת	
זֹאת עָמָל הִיא [הוּא]	
בְעֵינָי׃ **17** עַד־אָבוֹא אֶל־	
מִקְדְּשֵׁי־אֵל אָבִינָה	
לְאַחֲרִיתָם׃ **18** אַךְ בַּחֲלָקוֹת	
תָּשִׁית לָמוֹ הִפַּלְתָּם	
לְמַשּׁוּאוֹת׃ **19** אֵיךְ הָיוּ	
לְשַׁמָּה כְרָגַע סָפוּ תַמּוּ מִן־	
בַּלָּהוֹת׃ **20** כַּחֲלוֹם מֵהָקִיץ	
אֲדֹנָי בָּעִיר ׀ צַלְמָם תִּבְזֶה׃	
21 כִּי יִתְחַמֵּץ לְבָבִי וְכִלְיוֹתַי	
אֶשְׁתּוֹנָן׃ **22** וַאֲנִי־בַעַר וְלֹא	
אֵדַע בְּהֵמוֹת הָיִיתִי עִמָּךְ׃	
23 וַאֲנִי תָמִיד עִמָּךְ אָחַזְתָּ בְּיַד־	
יְמִינִי׃ **24** בַּעֲצָתְךָ תַנְחֵנִי	

23 Nevertheless *I am continually with You;

You have taken hold of my right hand.

24 With Your counsel You will *guide me,

And afterward *receive me [1]to glory.

Psa. 73:25 *Whom have I in heaven *but You?*

And [1]besides You, I desire nothing on earth.

26 My *flesh and my heart may fail,

But God is the [1]strength of my heart and my *portion forever.

27 For, behold, *those who are far from You will *perish;

You have [1]destroyed all those who [2c]are unfaithful to You.

28 But as for me, *the nearness of God is my good;

I have made the Lord [1]GOD my *refuge,

That I may *tell of all Your works.

וְאַחַר כָּבוֹד תִּקָּחֵנִי ׃ 25 מִי־

לִי בַשָּׁמָיִם וְעִמְּךָ לֹא־

חָפַצְתִּי בָאָרֶץ ׃ 26 כָּלָה

שְׁאֵרִי וּלְבָבִי צוּר־לְבָבִי

וְחֶלְקִי אֱלֹהִים לְעוֹלָם ׃ 27

כִּי־הִנֵּה רְחֵקֶיךָ יֹאבֵדוּ

הִצְמַתָּה כָּל־זוֹנֶה מִמֶּךָּ ׃ 28

וַאֲנִי ׀ קִרֲבַת אֱלֹהִים לִי־

טוֹב שַׁתִּי ׀ בַּאדֹנָי יְהוִֹה

מַחְסִי לְסַפֵּר כָּל־

מַלְאֲכוֹתֶיךָ ׃

References

Psalm 73:1
[a]Ps 86:5
[b]Ps 24:4; 51:10; Matt 5:8

Psalm 73:2
[1]Lit *were caused to slip*
[a]Ps 94:18

Psalm 73:3
[1]Or *boasters*
[a]Ps 37:1; Prov 23:17
[b]Job 21:7; Ps 37:7; Jer 12:1

Psalm 73:4
[1]Or *belly*

Psalm 73:5
[1]Lit *in the trouble of men*
[2]Or *mortals*
[3]Lit *with*
[a]Job 21:9; Ps 73:12
[b]Ps 73:14

Psalm 73:6
[a]Gen 41:42; Prov 1:9
[b]Ps 109:18

Psalm 73:7
[1]Lit *goes forth*
[2]Lit *overflow*
[a]Job 15:27; Ps 17:10; Jer 5:28

Psalm 73:8
[1]Or *they speak in wickedness; From on high they speak of oppression*
[a]Ps 1:1
[b]Ps 17:10; 2 Pet 2:18; Jude 16

Psalm 73:9
[1]Or *in*
[2]Lit *walks*
[a]Rev 13:6

Psalm 73:10
[1]Or *His*
[2]Lit *drained out*
[a]Ps 23:5

Psalm 73:11
[1]Lit *in*
[a]Job 22:13

Psalm 73:12
[a]Ps 49:6; 52:7
[b]Jer 49:31; Ezek 23:42

Psalm 73:13
[1]Or *cleansed my heart*
[a]Job 21:15; 34:9; 35:3
[b]Ps 26:6

Psalm 73:14
[1]Lit *my chastening*
[a]Ps 38:6
[b]Job 33:19; Ps 118:18

Psalm 73:15
[a]Ps 14:5

Psalm 73:16
[1]Lit *labor, trouble*
[a]Eccl 8:17

Psalm 73:17
[1]Lit *sanctuaries*
[a]Ps 27:4; 77:13
[b]Ps 37:38

Psalm 73:18

[1]Lit *ruins*
[a]Ps 35:6
[b]Ps 35:8; 36:12

Psalm 73:19
[1]Lit *become a desolation*
[a]Num 16:21; Is 47:11
[b]Job 18:11

Psalm 73:20
[1]Or *image*
[a]Job 20:8
[b]Ps 78:65
[c]1 Sam 2:30

Psalm 73:21
[1]Lit *in my kidneys*
[a]Judg 10:16
[b]Acts 2:37

Psalm 73:22
[1]Or *an animal*
[2]Lit *with You*
[a]Ps 49:10; 92:6
[b]Job 18:3; Ps 49:20; Eccl 3:18

Psalm 73:23
[a]Ps 16:8

Psalm 73:24
[1]Or *with honor*
[a]Ps 32:8; 48:14; Is 58:11
[b]Gen 5:24; Ps 49:15

Psalm 73:25
[1]Or *with*
[a]Ps 16:2; Phil 3:8

Psalm 73:26
[1]Lit *rock*
[a]Ps 38:10; 40:12; 84:2; 119:81

[b]Ps 16:5

Psalm 73:27

[1]Or *silenced*
[2]Lit *go to a whoring from*
[a]Ps 119:155
[b]Ps 37:20
[c]Ex 34:15; Num 15:39; Ps 106:39; Hos 4:12; 9:1

Psalm 73:28

[1]Heb *YHWH,* usually rendered *LORD*
[a]Ps 65:4; Heb 10:22; James 4:8
[b]Ps 14:6; 71:7
[c]Ps 40:5; 107:22; 118:17

Targum

Psa. 73:1 A psalm composed by Asaph. Truly, God is good to Israel, to the pure of heart. [2] But I – my feet had almost slipped; my steps had all but faltered. [3] For I became jealous of the mockers whenever I would see the welfare of the wicked. [4] For they are not dismayed and daunted by the day of their death; their opinions are sought out, and their heart is fat and strong. [5] They do not toil with the toil of men who are occupied with Torah; and they are not smitten with the righteous sons of men who endure sufferings. [6] Because of this, pride has adorned them, a crown that they place on their heads because of their rapacity. [7] Their faces are distorted by fat; their carvings have transgressed, the heart is ashamed. [8] They will decay because of fatness; and they will speak to cause harm and to oppress; they will speak from the arrogance of their heart. [9] They have set their mouth against the holy ones of heaven; and their tongue flares against the holy ones of the earth. [10] Then he turns against the people of the LORD, to rule them; and they will smite them with hammers, and cause many tears to flow from them. [11] And they will say, "How then does God know, and is there knowledge in the Most High?" [12] Behold, these are the wicked who dwell securely in this age; they have acquired property, they have procured wealth. [13] Truly, in vain have I purified my heart, and washed my hands in purity. [14] And I have been smitten all the day; and my admonition [has come] with every dawn. [15] If I said, "I will talk like them" – behold, I would have done evil to the generation of your children. [16] And I thought to know this, [but] it is a weariness in my sight – [17] Until the time of redemption, when I come to the sanctuaries of God, I will understand their fate. [18] Truly, you have placed them in dark places, you have thrown them into the wasteland. [19] How they have become a desolation in a moment! They are finished, destroyed because of chaos. [20] Like a dream of a man who awakes: the LORD in the great day of judgment, when they awake from their graves; in anger you will despise their likeness. [21] For my heart will feel pain, and my kidneys burn like fire. [22] And I am a fool, and I do not know; I was reckoned as a beast with you. [23] But I am continually with you; you have grasped my right hand. [24] You will guide me by your counsel; and after the glory that you commanded to come upon me is complete, you will take me. [25] Who, like you, is mine in heaven, but you? And besides you I desire no friend on earth. [26] My body and my heart are destroyed; God is the Mighty One who tries my heart and my portion forever. [27] For behold, the wicked who are far from you will perish; you have destroyed all who stray from the fear of you. [28] But I – to be near to the LORD is good to me; I have placed my confidence in the LORD God, to tell to all the righteous the commandments of your charge. --

Spiritual Awareness

Introduction

This Psalm is the first one of the third book of Psalms. The first two books deal with personal pleas, mainly from King David. The last two books are concerned with universal themes demonstrating the LORD's goodness. The introduction of this Psalm, an eloquent theme of the LORD, is always good to Israel. The psalmist surveyed Jewish history and beheld much misery for the LORD's people. At the same time, evil men flourished. Why does the way of the wicked prosper (Jeremiah 12:1)?

The writer Assaf said that everything the LORD does to Israel is good. The LORD caused suffering at times so that the fruits of good deeds may be preserved for the future world of reward. The sages Radak and Rashi agree.

Another view would be that the nations of the world were jealous that the LORD gave Israel the Promised Land and allowed the nation to prosper in the diaspora. The gentile nations of the world have tried for millennia to destroy Israel. However, the LORD would not let it happen.

Verse two

The author had almost turned away from the LORD. He had difficulty understanding the bad things that happened to Israel. Where is the LORD's justice when evil is snuffing out good? It is difficult to maintain faith in the LORD when persecution from the gentile nations is occurring.

But as for me, my feet had almost turned away, but little, and my steps would have been poured out.

Verse six

Evil men and women wear their evil as an ornament around their necks. This is seen today when certain people grab power in synagogues and churches. They forget that they should be concerned for the worship of the LORD and the betterment of the congregation. The leaders who grab power through evil will force the people to give them the respect they do not deserve and should not be given. The violence in synagogues and churches is passive-aggressive attitudes, backstabbing, and false gossip.

Therefore pride is the ornament around their necks; their form enwraps itself in violence.

Verse ten

Sadly, evil people show that they do not believe in the LORD. They grab their human authority and exploit it to get their way and power to control others. They take advantage of people by pretending to give them something good. Evil people convince good people to follow them.

Therefore, His people, too, turn thither again, and the waters of abundance will be tasted by them also.

Verse seventeen

Persons who accept and demonstrate the Torah shall become the bearers of the LORD's glory.

Until I entered into the sanctuaries of God and learned to look for their end, then I would become a bearer of the LORD's own glory.

Verse eighteen

Making a person's path smooth, the LORD let them fall prey to deceptions, to hopes remaining forever unfulfilled. The LORD places trouble in people's paths so that they can recognize evil when it confronts them. Suppose people believe that everything is positive and wonderful. In that case, they will be deceived by evil people and may commit evil themselves, thinking it is good. This is an answer to why bad things happen to good people.

You set them only on smooth places (and paths), but by doing so, You have let them fall prey to deception. Evil will overtake a person who does not experience what evil is.

Verse twenty-two

When a person's heart is embittered, their baser passions come to the surface.

Then I am a creature devoid of reason and shall not acquire understanding. So beast-like was I before You.

Psalm 74

New American Standard 1995	Hebrew
Psa. 74:0 A †Maskil of Asaph.	**Psa. 74:1** לָמָּה לְאָסָף מַשְׂכִּיל
Psa. 74:1 O God, why have You *a*rejected *us* forever?	יְעְשַׁן לָנֶצַח זָנַחְתָּ אֱלֹהִים
Why does Your anger *b*smoke against the *c*sheep of Your [1]pasture?	זְכֹר 2 : מַרְעִיתֶךָ בְּצֹאן אַפְּךָ
2 Remember Your congregation, which You have *a*purchased of old,	גָּאַלְתָּ קֶּדֶם קָנִיתָ וַ עֲדָתְךָ
Which You have *b*redeemed to be the *c*tribe of Your inheritance;	זֶה צִיּוֹן הַר נַחֲלָתֶךָ שֵׁבֶט
And this Mount *d*Zion, where You have dwelt.	פְּעָמֶיךָ הָרִימָה 3 : בּוֹ שָׁכַנְתָּ
3 [1]Turn Your footsteps toward the *a*perpetual ruins;	הָרַע כָל נֶצַח לְמַשֻּׁאוֹת
The enemy *b*has damaged everything within the sanctuary.	צֹרְרֶיךָ שָׁאֲגוּ 4 : בַּקֹּדֶשׁ אוֹיֵב
4 Your adversaries have *a*roared in the midst of Your meeting place;	אוֹתֹתָם שָׂמוּ מוֹעֲדֶךָ בְּקֶרֶב
They have set up their *b*own [1]standards *c*for signs.	כְּמֵבִיא יִוָּדַע 5 : אֹתוֹת
5 It seems as if one had lifted up	עֵץ בִסֲבָךְ לְמַעְלָה
His [1]*a*axe in a [2]forest of trees.	[עַתָּה][וְ] וְעֵת 6 : קַרְדֻּמּוֹת
6 And now [1]all its *a*carved work	בְּכַשִּׁיל יַחַד פִּתּוּחֶיהָ
They smash with hatchet and [2]hammers.	שִׁלְחוּ 7 : יַהֲלֹמוּן וְכֵילַפֹּת
7 They have [1]*a*burned Your sanctuary [2]to the ground;	חִלְּלוּ לָאָרֶץ מִקְדָּשֶׁךָ בָאֵשׁ
They have *b*defiled the dwelling place of Your name.	בְּלִבָּם אָמְרוּ 8 : שְׁמֶךָ מִשְׁכַּן
8 They *a*said in their heart, "Let us [1]completely [2]subdue them."	מוֹעֲדֵי כָל שָׂרְפוּ יַחַד נִינָם
They have burned all the meeting places of God in the land.	לֹא אוֹתֹתֵינוּ 9 : בָּאָרֶץ אֵל
9 We do not see our *a*signs;	וְלֹא נָבִיא עוֹד אֵין רָאִינוּ
There is *b*no longer any prophet,	עַד 10 : מָה עַד יֵדַע אִתָּנוּ

Nor is there any among us who knows *how long.

10   How long, O God, will the adversary *revile,

And the enemy *spurn Your name forever?

11   Why *do You withdraw Your hand, even Your right hand?

From within Your bosom, *destroy *them!*

Psa. 74:12   Yet God is *my king from of old,

Who works deeds of deliverance in the midst of the earth.

13   [1]You *divided the sea by Your strength;

[1]You *broke the heads of the *sea monsters [2]in the waters.

14   [1]You crushed the heads of [2a]Leviathan;

[1]You gave him as food for the [3]creatures *of the wilderness.

15   [1]You *broke open springs and torrents;

[1]You *dried up ever-flowing streams.

16   Yours is the day, Yours also is the night;

[1]You have *prepared the [2]light and the sun.

17   [1]You have *established all the boundaries of the earth;

[1]You have [2]made *summer and winter.

Psa. 74:18   Remember this, [1]O LORD, that the enemy has *reviled,

And a *foolish people has spurned Your name.

מָתַי אֱלֹהִים יְחָרֶף צָר יְנָאֵץ
אוֹיֵב שִׁמְךָ לָנֶצַח׃ 11 לָמָה
תָשִׁיב יָדְךָ וִימִינֶךָ מִקֶּרֶב
חוֹקְךָ [חֵיקְךָ] כַלֵּה׃ 12
וֵאלֹהִים מַלְכִּי מִקֶּדֶם פֹּעֵל
יְשׁוּעוֹת בְּקֶרֶב הָאָרֶץ׃ 13
אַתָּה פוֹרַרְתָּ בְעָזְּךָ יָם
שִׁבַּרְתָּ רָאשֵׁי תַנִּינִים עַל־
הַמָּיִם׃ 14 אַתָּה רִצַּצְתָּ רָאשֵׁי
לִוְיָתָן תִּתְּנֶנּוּ מַאֲכָל לְעָם
לְצִיִּים׃ 15 אַתָּה בָקַעְתָּ מַעְיָן
וָנָחַל אַתָּה הוֹבַשְׁתָּ נַהֲרוֹת
אֵיתָן׃ 16 לְךָ יוֹם אַף־לְךָ
לָיְלָה אַתָּה הֲכִינוֹתָ מָאוֹר
וָשָׁמֶשׁ׃ 17 אַתָּה הִצַּבְתָּ כָּל־
גְּבוּלוֹת אָרֶץ קַיִץ וָחֹרֶף
אַתָּה יְצַרְתָּם׃ 18 זְכָר־זֹאת
אוֹיֵב חֵרֵף ׀ יְהוָה וְעַם נָבָל
נִאֲצוּ שְׁמֶךָ׃ 19 אַל־תִּתֵּן
לְחַיַּת נֶפֶשׁ תּוֹרֶךָ חַיַּת עֲנִיֶּיךָ
אַל־תִּשְׁכַּח לָנֶצַח׃ 20 הַבֵּט
לַבְּרִית כִּי מָלְאוּ מַחֲשַׁכֵּי־
אֶרֶץ נְאוֹת חָמָס׃ 21 אַל־יָשֹׁב

19 Do not deliver the soul of Your [a]turtledove to the wild beast;

[b]Do not forget the life of Your afflicted forever.

20 Consider the [a]covenant;

For the [b]dark places of the land are full of the habitations of violence.

21 Let not the [a]oppressed return dishonored;

Let the [b]afflicted and needy praise Your name.

Psa. 74:22 Arise, O God, *and* [a]plead Your own cause;

Remember [1]how the [b]foolish man reproaches You all day long.

23 Do not forget the voice of Your [a]adversaries,

The [b]uproar of those who rise against You which ascends continually.

בָּ֣ךְ נִכְלָ֑ם עָנִ֥י וְ֝אֶבְי֗וֹן יְֽהַֽלְל֥וּ שְׁמֶֽךָ׃ 22 קוּמָ֣ה אֱ֭לֹהִים רִיבָ֣ה רִיבֶ֑ךָ זְכֹ֥ר חֶרְפָּתְךָ֥ מִנִּי־נָ֝בָ֗ל כָּל־הַיּֽוֹם׃ 23 אַל־תִּ֭שְׁכַּח ק֣וֹל צֹרְרֶ֑יךָ שְׁא֥וֹן קָ֝מֶ֗יךָ עֹלֶ֥ה תָמִֽיד׃

References

Psalm 74:0
†Possibly, *Contemplative,* or *Didactic,* or *Skillful Psalm*

Psalm 74:1
[1]Or *pasturing*
[a]Ps 44:9; 77:7
[b]Deut 29:20; Ps 18:8; 89:46
[c]Ps 79:13; 95:7; 100:3

Psalm 74:2
[a]Ex 15:16; Deut 32:6
[b]Ex 15:13; Ps 77:15; 106:10; Is 63:9
[c]Deut 32:9; Is 63:17; Jer 10:16; 51:19
[d]Ps 9:11; 68:16

Psalm 74:3
[1]Lit *Lift up*
[a]Is 61:4
[b]Ps 79:1

Psalm 74:4
[1]Lit *signs*
[a]Lam 2:7
[b]Num 2:2
[c]Ps 74:9

Psalm 74:5
[1]Lit *axes*
[2]Lit *thicket*
[a]Jer 46:22

Psalm 74:6
[1]Lit *altogether*
[2]Or *axes*
[a]1 Kin 6:18, 29, 32, 35

Psalm 74:7
[1]Lit *set on fire*

[2]Or *To the ground they...*
[a]2 Kin 25:9
[b]Ps 89:39; Lam 2:2

Psalm 74:8
[1]Lit *altogether*
[2]Or *oppress*
[a]Ps 83:4

Psalm 74:9
[a]Ps 78:43
[b]1 Sam 3:1; Lam 2:9; Ezek 7:26; Amos 8:11
[c]Ps 6:3; 79:5; 80:4

Psalm 74:10
[a]Ps 44:16; 79:12; 89:51
[b]Lev 24:16

Psalm 74:11
[a]Lam 2:3
[b]Ps 59:13

Psalm 74:12
[a]Ps 44:4

Psalm 74:13
[1]Or *You Yourself*
[2]Lit *on*
[a]Ex 14:21; Ps 78:13
[b]Is 51:9
[c]Ps 148:7; Jer 51:34

Psalm 74:14
[1]Or *You Yourself*
[2]Or *sea monster*
[3]Lit *people*
[a]Job 41:1; Ps 104:26; Is 27:1
[b]Ps 72:9

Psalm 74:15
[1]Or *You Yourself*

[a]Ex 17:5, 6; Num 20:11; Ps 78:15; 105:41; 114:8; Is 48:21
[b]Ex 14:21, 22; Josh 2:10; 3:13; Ps 114:3

Psalm 74:16
[1]Or *You Yourself*
[2]Or *luminary*
[a]Gen 1:14-18; Ps 104:19; 136:7, 8

Psalm 74:17
[1]Or *You Yourself*
[2]Or *formed*
[a]Deut 32:8; Acts 17:26
[b]Gen 8:22; Ps 147:16-18

Psalm 74:18
[1]Or *that the enemy has reviled the LORD*
[a]Ps 74:10
[b]Deut 32:6; Ps 14:1; 39:8; 53:1

Psalm 74:19
[a]Song 2:14
[b]Ps 9:18

Psalm 74:20
[a]Gen 17:7; Ps 106:45
[b]Ps 88:6; 143:3

Psalm 74:21
[a]Ps 103:6
[b]Ps 35:10; Is 41:17

Psalm 74:22
[1]Lit *Your reproach from the foolish man*
[a]Ps 43:1; Is 3:13; 43:26; Ezek 20:35
[b]Ps 14:1; 53:1; 74:18

Psalm 74:23
[a]Ps 74:10
[b]Ps 65:7

Targum

Psa. 74:1 A good lesson, composed by Asaph. Why, O God, have you moved far off forever? [Why] will your anger be fierce against the flock of your pasture? ² Remember your congregation that you acquired of old; you redeemed from Egypt the tribes of your inheritance, this same Mount Zion on which you made your presence to abide. ³ Lift up your footsteps to dissolve the nations forever, for the enemy with all his strength has done harm in the holy place. ⁴ Your oppressors cry out in the midst of your assemblies; they have set up their standards as signs. ⁵ He will strike with a hammer like a man who lifts up his hand against a wood thicket to cut it with axes. ⁶ But now they pull down its carvings together; they pound with the hatchet and the two-edged chisel as if with mallets. ⁷ They have burned the sanctuary to the ground with fire; they have defiled the tabernacle in which your name is uttered. ⁸ Their children spoke in their hearts together; their fathers burned all the assemblies of God in the land. ⁹ We have not seen our signs that the prophets gave us; there are no longer any prophets and we have none with us who knows how long. ¹⁰ How long, O God, will the oppressor show disdain? Will the enemy reject your name forever? ¹¹ Why will you withdraw your hand, even your right hand, from redeeming? Take it out of your bosom and do away with oppression. ¹² But God is the king, whose holy presence is from of old, one who carries out redemption in the midst of the land. ¹³ You cut off the waters of the sea by your power; you broke the heads of the sea serpents, and drowned the Egyptians at the sea. ¹⁴ You shattered the heads of Pharaoh's warriors; you handed them over for destruction to the people of the house of Israel, and their corpses to jackals. ¹⁵ You split the spring from the rock and it became a stream; you dried up the ford of the streams of the Arnon and the ford of the Jabbok and the Jordan, which were so powerful. ¹⁶ Yours is the day-time, yours, too, is the night; you have made firm the moon and sun. ¹⁷ You set up all the boundaries of the earth; summer and winter, you created them. ¹⁸ Remember this, the enemy, slanderer of the LORD, and the foolish people who have rejected your name. ¹⁹ Do not deliver the souls of those who teach your Torah to the Gentiles, who are likened to beasts of the field; do not forget the lives of your poor forever. ²⁰ Look at the covenant that you made with our fathers, for their children are finished off; darkness is spread over the land, and fraud, and violence. ²¹ The pauper will not return ashamed; the poor and lowly will praise your name. ²² Arise, O God; argue your case; call to mind the disgrace of your people because of foolish counsel all the day. ²³ Do not forget the voice of your oppressors, the turmoil, always mounting, of those who stand against you.

Spiritual Awareness

Introduction

The question of why righteous people suffer was covered in Psalm 73. The Psalmist studies the most painful example of the apparent injustice, the pitiful flight of the Jews in Exile. Assaf, the Psalmist, protested against the strictness of the LORD's judgment and questioned its equity. The LORD told Assaf that it was the Jews who abandoned Him when they stopped following the Torah. The Ten Commandments state that the LORD will watch over Israel if they follow the LORD's Torah.

Verse four

The Psalmist reminds the LORD that it was the enemies of Him who invaded and destroyed His Temple in Jerusalem. This is important to understand today. Many members and attendees of synagogues and churches are proving to be the enemies of the institution and, thus, enemies of the LORD. The people must believe in the LORD's ways and treat each other with respect and love. When people play power games for their own glory, they sully the name of the LORD.

It was as Your oppressors raged in the midst of Your meeting place; they have set up their signs as signs.

Verse eight

The enemies of the LORD who destroyed the Temple did so that the Jewish people would abandon the LORD. People in synagogue and church who strive for power for themselves and not for the LORD are doing the same thing the Babylonians did. They are burning down the LORD's meeting place. How many synagogues and churches have closed because power struggles overtook worship to the LORD? It is a large number. The infighting within Christian denominations has caused membership drops. When members realize that their leaders are in it for themselves, they leave. Many stop attending a synagogue or church because they believe they will find the same situation in the new place similar to the situation they left. If this continues, our future generations will not have places to worship and will thus not learn about the LORD.

They have said in their heart, "Their future generations, altogether." Thus they have burned up all the meeting places of God upon the earth.

Verse twenty-one

The Psalmist asks the LORD to answer a plea for help from the poor and powerless. He prays for intervention on their behalf. He also prays for the tyrants of the world to be crushed. Tyrants do not follow the Laws and Ways of the Torah. The poor and powerless should be protected and not exploited in the past, the present, or the future.

O let the crushed one not turn back in shame. Give the poor and defenseless cause to proclaim the praise of Your Name.

Psalm 75

New American Standard 1995	Hebrew
Psa. 75:0 For the choir director; *set to* †Al-tashheth. A Psalm of Asaph, a Song. **Psa. 75:1** We *a*give thanks to You, O God, we give thanks, For Your name is *b*near; Men declare *c*Your wondrous works. 2 "When I select an *a*appointed time, It is I who *b*judge with equity. 3 "The *a*earth and all who dwell in it [1]melt; It is I who have firmly set its *b*pillars. [2]Selah. 4 "I said to the boastful, 'Do not boast,' And to the wicked, *c*'Do not lift up the horn; 5 Do not lift up your horn on high, *a*'Do not speak with insolent [1]pride.'" **Psa. 75:6** For not from the east, nor from the west, Nor from the [1a]desert *comes* exaltation; 7 But *a*God is the Judge; He *b*puts down one and exalts another. 8 For a *a*cup is in the hand of the LORD, and the wine foams; It is [1b]well mixed, and He pours out of this; Surely all the wicked of the earth must drain *and* *c*drink down its dregs.	**Psa. 75:1** לַמְנַצֵּחַ אַל־תַּשְׁחֵת מִזְמוֹר לְאָסָף שִׁיר׃ 2 הוֹדִינוּ לְּךָ ׀ אֱלֹהִים הוֹדִינוּ וְקָרוֹב שְׁמֶךָ סִפְּרוּ נִפְלְאוֹתֶיךָ׃ 3 כִּי אֶקַּח מוֹעֵד אֲנִי מֵישָׁרִים אֶשְׁפֹּט׃ 4 נְמֹגִים אֶרֶץ וְכָל־יֹשְׁבֶיהָ אָנֹכִי תִכַּנְתִּי עַמּוּדֶיהָ סֶּלָה׃ 5 אָמַרְתִּי לַהוֹלְלִים אַל־תָּהֹלּוּ וְלָרְשָׁעִים אַל־תָּרִימוּ קָרֶן׃ 6 אַל־תָּרִימוּ לַמָּרוֹם קַרְנְכֶם תְּדַבְּרוּ בְצַוָּאר עָתָק׃ 7 כִּי לֹא מִמּוֹצָא וּמִמַּעֲרָב וְלֹא מִמִּדְבַּר הָרִים׃ 8 כִּי־אֱלֹהִים שֹׁפֵט זֶה יַשְׁפִּיל וְזֶה יָרִים׃ 9 כִּי כוֹס בְּיַד־יְהוָה וְיַיִן חָמַר מָלֵא מֶסֶךְ וַיַּגֵּר מִזֶּה אַךְ־שְׁמָרֶיהָ יִמְצוּ יִשְׁתּוּ כֹּל רִשְׁעֵי־אָרֶץ׃ 10 וַאֲנִי אַגִּיד

Psa. 75:9   But as for me, I will *a*declare *it* forever;

I will sing praises to the God of Jacob.

10   And all the *a*horns of the wicked [1]He will cut off,

But *b*the horns of the righteous will be lifted up.

לְעֹלָם אֲזַמְּרָה לֵאלֹהֵי יַעֲקֹב ׃ וְכָל־קַרְנֵי רְשָׁעִים אֲגַדֵּעַ תְּרוֹמַמְנָה קַרְנוֹת צַדִּיק ׃

References

Psalm 75:0
[†]Lit *Do Not Destroy*

Psalm 75:1
[a]Ps 79:13
[b]Ps 145:18
[c]Ps 26:7; 44:1; 71:17

Psalm 75:2
[a]Ps 102:13
[b]Ps 9:8; 67:4; Is 11:4

Psalm 75:3
[1]Or *totter*
[2]*Selah* may mean: *Pause, Crescendo* or *Musical interlude*
[a]Ps 46:6; Is 24:19
[b]1 Sam 2:8

Psalm 75:4
[a]Zech 1:21

Psalm 75:5
[1]Lit *neck*
[a]1 Sam 2:3; Ps 94:4

Psalm 75:6
[1]Or *mountainous desert*
[a]Ps 3:3

Psalm 75:7
[a]Ps 50:6
[b]1 Sam 2:7; Ps 147:6; Dan 2:21

Psalm 75:8
[1]Lit *full of mixture*
[a]Job 21:20; Ps 11:6; 60:3; Jer 25:15
[b]Prov 23:30
[c]Obad 16

Psalm 75:9

*Ps 22:22; 40:10

Psalm 75:10

[1]Heb *I*

*Ps 101:8; Jer 48:25

[b]1 Sam 2:1; Ps 89:17; 92:10; 148:14

Targum

Psa. 75:1 For praise; in the time that David said, "Do not harm your people." A psalm composed by Asaph, and a song. [2] We have praised you, O LORD, we have praised you, and your name is near, your wonders have declared it. [3] Because of the meeting of the festival, I will judge uprightly. [4] The inhabitants of the earth melt away, and all who dwell in it; I have made its pillars firm forever. [5] I said to the mockers, "Do not mock," and to the wicked, "Do not exalt [your] honor." [6] Do not exalt your honor to the height, you who speak in harshness and blasphemy. [7] For there is none beside me from east to west, nor from the north, the area of deserts, to the south, the site of mountains. [8] For God is a righteous judge; this one he will humble, and this one he will exalt. [9] For the cup of cursing is in the hand of the LORD, and a harsh wine, full of a bitter mixture, to confuse the wits of the wicked by what is poured out from it, and more severe than the judgment of the ancients; yet its dregs and its foam all the wicked of the earth will press out and drink. [10] But I will tell forever the miracles; I will praise the God of Jacob. [11] But all the mighty loftiness of the wicked I will humble; I will uproot them from their strongholds; the mighty loftiness of the righteous will be magnified.

Spiritual Awareness

Introduction

Even though the Babylonian Exile did come to a close, many Hebrew people lived outside the Promised Land. This situation is considered an exile for the Jewish people. The problems for Israel are going to mount in rapid succession. At the end of time, a battle between Gog and Magog will encompass the globe. Trampled and terrified, Israel will turn to the LORD for salvation. The LORD will respond with the assurance that salvation is imminent. It is the LORD who will decide when the waiting time for the restoration of Israel will occur.

Verse one

The Psalmist calls out to the Sefirah Netzach to grant victory for Israel when the destruction of the world comes.

To the Sefirah Netzach who grants victory. Stop the destruction of the world. A psalm, a song of Asaf.

Verse two

Human greatness consists of two concepts. The first is the "hand" with which humans rule over the earth. The second is "perception," which is the power in the spiritual sense of the word.

We have rendered You homage, O God, we have rendered homage, and Your name is near to us still; Your wondrous works have recounted it.

Verse four

Even though the earth and all its inhabitants' despair, I have established its pillars with deliberation. Meditate on this verse.

Verse six

Suppose you set yourself above your fellow person because of your contempt for the Torah. In that case, you set yourself above the LORD by presuming to despise Him and trample His Law underfoot.

Metaphorical translation - Lift not your horn heavenward by speaking insolence with a haughty neck.

Spiritual translation – Do not let yourself be in contempt of the Torah because you are showing hatred for the LORD.

Verse nine

When the LORD determines a person's fate, He considers not only his past or present but, most of all, his future needs.

Metaphorical translation - For there is a cup in the hand of God, the wine has ceased to ferment, but it is full of a mixture when He pours out from it. All the lawless of the earth shall drain and drink only the dregs.

Spiritual translation - When the LORD determines a person's fate, He takes into account not only his past or present but also his future needs.

Verse ten

The righteous will be rewarded, and the wicked will get what they deserve.

Psalm 76

New American Standard 1995	Hebrew
Psa. 76:0 For the choir director; on stringed instruments. A Psalm of Asaph, a Song.	לַמְנַצֵּחַ בִּנְגִינֹת **Psa. 76:1**
Psa. 76:1 God is [a]known in Judah; His name is [b]great in Israel.	מִזְמוֹר לְאָסָף שִׁיר ׃ 2 נוֹדָע
2 His [1a]tabernacle is in [b]Salem; His [c]dwelling place also is in Zion.	בִּיהוּדָה אֱלֹהִים בְּיִשְׂרָאֵל
3 There He [a]broke the [1]flaming arrows, The shield and the sword and the [2]weapons of war. [3]Selah.	גָּדוֹל שְׁמוֹ ׃ 3 וַיְהִי בְשָׁלֵם
	סֻכּוֹ וּמְעוֹנָתוֹ בְצִיּוֹן ׃ 4 שָׁמָּה
Psa. 76:4 You are resplendent, [1]More majestic than the mountains of prey.	שִׁבַּר רִשְׁפֵי־קָשֶׁת מָגֵן וְחֶרֶב
5 The [a]stouthearted were plundered, [1]They sank into sleep; And none of the [2]warriors could use his hands.	וּמִלְחָמָה סֶלָה ׃ 5 נָאוֹר אַתָּה
6 At Your [a]rebuke, O God of Jacob, Both [1b]rider and horse were cast into a dead sleep.	אַדִּיר מֵהַרְרֵי־טָרֶף ׃ 6
7 You, even You, are [a]to be feared; And [b]who may stand in Your presence when once [1]You are angry?	אֶשְׁתּוֹלְלוּ ׀ אַבִּירֵי לֵב נָמוּ
	שְׁנָתָם וְלֹא־מָצְאוּ כָל־
Psa. 76:8 You caused judgment to be heard from heaven; The earth [a]feared and was still	אַנְשֵׁי־חַיִל יְדֵיהֶם ׃ 7
9 When God [a]arose to judgment, To save all the humble of the earth. Selah.	מִגַּעֲרָתְךָ אֱלֹהֵי יַעֲקֹב נִרְדָּם
10 For the [1a]wrath of man shall praise You;	וְרֶכֶב וָסוּס ׃ 8 אַתָּה ׀ נוֹרָא
	אַתָּה וּמִי־יַעֲמֹד לְפָנֶיךָ מֵאָז
	אַפֶּךָ ׃ 9 מִשָּׁמַיִם הִשְׁמַעְתָּ דִּין
	אֶרֶץ יָרְאָה וְשָׁקָטָה ׃ 10
	בְּקוּם־לַמִּשְׁפָּט אֱלֹהִים
	לְהוֹשִׁיעַ כָּל־עַנְוֵי־אֶרֶץ
	סֶלָה ׃ 11 כִּי־חֲמַת אָדָם

<table>
<tr><td>

With a remnant of wrath You will gird Yourself.

Psa. 76:11 [a]Make vows to the LORD your God and [b]fulfill *them;*

Let all who are around Him [c]bring gifts to Him who is to be feared.

12 He will cut off the spirit of princes;

He is [1a]feared by the kings of the earth.

</td><td>

תּוֹדֶךָ שְׁאֵרִית חֵמֹת תַּחְגֹּר ׃
נִדְרוּ וְשַׁלְּמוּ לַיהוָה 12
אֱלֹהֵיכֶם כָּל־סְבִיבָיו יוֹבִילוּ
שַׁי לַמּוֹרָא ׃ 13 יִבְצֹר רוּחַ
נְגִידִים נוֹרָא לְמַלְכֵי־אָרֶץ ׃

</td></tr>
</table>

References

Psalm 76:1
[a]Ps 48:3
[b]Ps 99:3

Psalm 76:2
[1]Lit *shelter*
[a]Ps 27:5; Lam 2:6
[b]Gen 14:18
[c]Ps 9:11; 132:13; 135:21

Psalm 76:3
[1]Lit *fiery shafts of the bow*
[2]Lit *battle*
[3]*Selah* may mean: *Pause, Crescendo* or *Musical interlude*
[a]Ps 46:9

Psalm 76:4
[1]Or *Majestic from the mountains*

Psalm 76:5
[1]Lit *They slumbered their sleep*
[2]Lit *men of might have found their hands*
[a]Is 10:12; 46:12

Psalm 76:6
[1]Lit *chariot*
[a]Ps 80:16
[b]Ex 15:1, 21; Ps 78:53

Psalm 76:7
[1]Lit *Your anger is*
[a]1 Chr 16:25; Ps 89:7; 96:4
[b]Ezra 9:15; Ps 130:3; Nah 1:6; Mal 3:2; Rev 6:17

Psalm 76:8
[a]1 Chr 16:30; 2 Chr 20:29, 30; Ps 33:8

Psalm 76:9

[a]Ps 9:7, 8; 74:22; 82:8

Psalm 76:10
[1]Lit *wraths*
[a]Ex 9:16; Rom 9:17

Psalm 76:11
[a]Eccl 5:4-6
[b]Ps 50:14
[c]2 Chr 32:23; Ps 68:29

Psalm 76:12
[1]Lit *awesome to*
[a]Ps 47:2

Targum

Psa. 76:1 For praise, as a psalm; a psalm composed by Asaph, a song. ² God has become known among those of the house of Judah; his name is great among those of the house of Israel. ³ And his sanctuary has come to be in Jerusalem, and the dwelling of the house of his holy presence is in Zion. ⁴ When the house of Israel did his will, he made his presence abide among them; there he broke the arrows and bows of the Gentiles who were making war; he made forever the shields and battle-lines of no account. ⁵ Bright [and] awful are you, O God, acclaimed from your sanctuary; the kings who dwell in the mountain fortresses, the place where their spoil is gathered, will tremble in your presence. ⁶ The mighty in heart have stripped from them the weapons of war; they have slumbered in their sleep; and all the men of might have not been able to grasp their weapons in their hands. ⁷ At your rebuke, O God of Jacob, the chariots have fallen asleep, and the cavalry have been disabled. ⁸ You are awesome, you are God; and who will stand before you from the time your anger becomes strong? ⁹ From heaven you proclaimed judgment on the land of the Gentiles; the land of Israel was afraid [and] became silent. ¹⁰ The righteous say, "Let God arise for judgment with the wicked, to redeem from their hands all the meek of the earth forever." ¹¹ When you are angry at your people, you show mercy to them, and they will give thanks to your name; but the remainder of fury that is left to you, out of the wrath that you showed, you will gird on to destroy the Gentiles. [ANOTHER TARGUM: For when your anger grows strong against your people, they will repent and give thanks to your name, and you turn from anger; but against the remnant of the Gentiles you will gird on the instruments of anger.] ¹² Make vows and fulfill [them] in the presence of the LORD your God, all you who dwell around his sanctuary; let them bring offerings to his awesome temple. ¹³ He will diminish the arrogant spirits of the leaders; [he is] dreadful to all the kings of the earth.

Spiritual Awareness

Introduction

The LORD's majesty is now concealed in the shrouds of exile. The future triumph of the LORD over Gog and Magog will signal the return of Divine prestige. The LORD's glory will gradually spread until it is recognized worldwide. Divine protection will envelop Jerusalem, the LORD's dwelling place.

Verse one

To the Sefirah Netzach who grants victory through the art of music, a psalm, a song of Asaf.

Verse three

The original name of Jerusalem was Salem. Jerusalem is on the top of Mount Zion.

When His tabernacle was in Salem and His dwelling-place in Zion.

Verse ten

When God arises to judgment, it is to bring salvation to all the humble of the earth. Meditate on this verse.

Verse twelve

Midrash says that every Jewish soul that will ever live on the earth was in the valley of Mount Sinai when the LORD asked the people if they would accept His Torah. When they accepted the Torah the LORD said that he would always protect them. This is the vow of all Jewish people.

But as far as you, vow, and fulfill your vows to the LORD your God, while all those round about Him bring tribute to Him as to One to be revered.

Psalm 77

New American Standard 1995	Hebrew

Psa. 77:0 For the choir director; †according to Jeduthun. A Psalm of Asaph.

Psa. 77:1 My voice *rises* to God, and I will [a]cry aloud;

My voice *rises* to God, and He will hear me.

2 In the [a]day of my trouble I sought the Lord;

[b]In the night my [c]hand was stretched out [1]without weariness;

My soul [d]refused to be comforted.

3 *When* I remember God, then I am [a]disturbed;

When I [b]sigh, then [c]my spirit grows faint. [1]Selah.

4 You have held my eyelids *open*;

I am so troubled that I [a]cannot speak.

5 I have considered the [a]days of old,

The years of long ago.

6 I will remember my [a]song in the night;

I [b]will meditate with my heart,

And my spirit [1]ponders:

Psa. 77:7 Will the Lord [a]reject forever?

And will He [b]never be favorable again?

8 Has His [a]lovingkindness ceased forever?

Has *His* [1b]promise come to an end [2]forever?

9 Has God [a]forgotten to be gracious,

לַמְנַצֵּחַ עַל־יְדִיתוּן **Psa. 77:1**

[יְדוּתוּן] לְאָסָף מִזְמוֹר ‎2 :

קוֹלִי אֶל־אֱלֹהִים וְאֶצְעָקָה

קוֹלִי אֶל־אֱלֹהִים וְהַאֲזִין

אֵלָי ‎3 : בְּיוֹם צָרָתִי אֲדֹנָי

דָּרָשְׁתִּי יָדִי ׀ לַיְלָה נִגְּרָה

וְלֹא תָפוּג מֵאֲנָה הִנָּחֵם

נַפְשִׁי ‎4 : אֶזְכְּרָה אֱלֹהִים

וְאֶהֱמָיָה אָשִׂיחָה ׀ וְתִתְעַטֵּף

רוּחִי סֶלָה ‎5 : אָחַזְתָּ שְׁמֻרוֹת

עֵינָי נִפְעַמְתִּי וְלֹא אֲדַבֵּר ‎6 :

חִשַּׁבְתִּי יָמִים מִקֶּדֶם שְׁנוֹת

עוֹלָמִים ‎7 : אֶזְכְּרָה נְגִינָתִי

בַּלַּיְלָה עִם־לְבָבִי אָשִׂיחָה

וַיְחַפֵּשׂ רוּחִי ‎8 : הַלְעוֹלָמִים

יִזְנַח ׀ אֲדֹנָי וְלֹא־יֹסִיף

לִרְצוֹת עוֹד ‎9 : הֶאָפֵס לָנֶצַח

חַסְדּוֹ גָּמַר אֹמֶר לְדֹר וָדֹר ‎:

הֲשָׁכַח חַנּוֹת אֵל אִם־קָפַץ ‎10

Or has He in anger [1]withdrawn His [b]compassion? Selah.

10   Then I said, "It is my [1]grief,
That the [b]right hand of the Most High has changed."

Psa. 77:11   I shall remember the [a]deeds of [1]the LORD;
Surely I will [a]remember Your wonders of old.

12   I will [a]meditate on all Your work
And muse on Your deeds.

13   Your way, O God, is [a]holy;
[b]What God is great like our God?

14   You are the [a]God who works wonders;
You have [b]made known Your strength among the peoples.

15   You have by Your [1]power [a]redeemed Your people,
The sons of Jacob and [b]Joseph. Selah.

Psa. 77:16   The [a]waters saw You, O God;
The waters saw You, they were in anguish;
The deeps also trembled.

17   The [a]clouds poured out water;
The skies [b]gave forth a sound;
Your [c]arrows [1]flashed here and there.

18   The [a]sound of Your thunder was in the whirlwind;
The [b]lightnings lit up the world;
The [c]earth trembled and shook.

19   Your [a]way was in the sea
And Your paths in the mighty waters,
And Your footprints may not be known.

11 וַיֹּאמֶר : בְּאַף רַחֲמָיו סֶלָה
יְמִין שְׁנוֹת הִיא חַלּוֹתִי
[אֶזְכּוֹר] אַזְכִּיר 12 : עֶלְיוֹן
אֶזְכְּרָה כִי־יָהּ מַעֲלְלֵי־
וְהָגִיתִי 13 : פִלְאֶךָ מִקֶּדֶם
בַעֲלִילוֹתֶיךָ וּבְכָל־פָּעֳלֶךָ
בַּקֹּדֶשׁ אֱלֹהִים 14 : אָשִׂיחָה
גָּדוֹל מִי־אֵל דַּרְכֶּךָ
הָאֵל אַתָּה 15 : כֵאלֹהִים
בָעַמִּים הוֹדַעְתָּ פֶלֶא עֹשֵׂה
עַמְּךָ בִזְרוֹעַ גָּאַלְתָּ 16 : עֻזֶּךָ
17 : סֶלָה וְיוֹסֵף בְנֵי־יַעֲקֹב
רָאוּךָ אֱלֹהִים מַּיִם רָאוּךָ
יָרְגְּזוּ אַף יָחִילוּ מַּיִם
עָבוֹת מַיִם זֹרְמוּ 18 : תְּהֹמוֹת
אַף־ שְׁחָקִים נָתְנוּ קוֹל
קוֹל 19 : יִתְהַלָּכוּ חֲצָצֶיךָ
הֵאִירוּ בַגַּלְגַּל רַעַמְךָ
וַתִּרְעַשׁ רָגְזָה תֵבֵל בְּרָקִים
דַּרְכֶּךָ בַּיָּם 20 : הָאָרֶץ
בְּמַיִם [וּשְׁבִילְךָ] וּשְׁבִילְךָ
נֹדָעוּ לֹא וְעִקְּבוֹתֶיךָ רַבִּים

| 20 | You ᵃled Your people like a flock
By the hand of ᵇMoses and Aaron. | 21 נָחִיתָ כַצֹּאן עַמֶּךָ בְּיַד־
מֹשֶׁה וְאַהֲרֹן׃ |

References

Psalm 77:0
[†]1 Chr 16:41

Psalm 77:1
[a]Ps 3:4; 142:1

Psalm 77:2
[1]Lit *and did not grow numb*
[a]Ps 50:15; 86:7
[b]Ps 63:6; Is 26:9
[c]Job 11:13; Ps 88:9
[d]Gen 37:35

Psalm 77:3
[1]*Selah* may mean: *Pause, Crescendo* or *Musical interlude*
[a]Ps 42:5, 11; 43:5
[b]Ps 55:2; 142:2
[c]Ps 61:2; 143:4

Psalm 77:4
[a]Ps 39:9

Psalm 77:5
[a]Deut 32:7; Ps 44:1; 143:5; Is 51:9

Psalm 77:6
[1]Lit *searched*
[a]Ps 42:8
[b]Ps 4:4

Psalm 77:7
[a]Ps 44:9
[b]Ps 85:1, 5

Psalm 77:8
[1]Lit *word*
[2]Lit *from generation to generation*
[a]Ps 89:49

[b]2 Pet 3:9

Psalm 77:9
[1]Lit *shut up*
[a]Is 49:15
[b]Ps 25:6; 40:11; 51:1

Psalm 77:10
[1]Or *infirmity, the years of the right hand of the Most High*
[a]Ps 31:22; 73:14
[b]Ps 44:2, 3

Psalm 77:11
[1]Heb *YAH*
[a]Ps 105:5; 143:5

Psalm 77:12
[a]Ps 145:5

Psalm 77:13
[a]Ps 63:2; 73:17
[b]Ex 15:11; Ps 71:19; 86:8

Psalm 77:14
[a]Ps 72:18
[b]Ps 106:8

Psalm 77:15
[1]Lit *arm*
[a]Ex 6:6; Deut 9:29; Ps 74:2; 78:42
[b]Ps 80:1

Psalm 77:16
[a]Ex 14:21; Ps 114:3; Hab 3:8, 10

Psalm 77:17
[1]Lit *went*
[a]Judg 5:4
[b]Ps 68:33
[c]Ps 18:14

Psalm 77:18
*a*Ps 18:13; 104:7
*b*Ps 97:4
*c*Judg 5:4; Ps 18:7

Psalm 77:19
*a*Is 51:10; Hab 3:15

Psalm 77:20
*a*Ex 13:21; 14:19; Ps 78:52; 80:1; Is 63:11-13
*b*Ex 6:26; Ps 105:26

Targum

Psa. 77:1 For praise; composed by Jeduthun for Asaph; a psalm. ² My voice is [raised] in the presence of the LORD, and I will complain; my voice is [raised] in the presence of God; hear my utterance! ³ In the day of my distress, I sought instruction from the presence of the LORD; the spirit of prophecy rested on me in the night; my eye ran with tears and will not stop; my soul refused to be comforted. ⁴ I will remember God and I will tremble in the presence of the LORD; I will speak, and my spirit will be weary forever. ⁵ You have shut the lids of my eyes; I am smitten, and I will not speak. ⁶ I have counted up the good days which were at the beginning, the good years of long ago. ⁷ I will remember my Psalm in the night; I will speak with the thoughts of my heart, and the mind of my spirit will examine miracles. ⁸ Can the LORD be far off forever, and no longer show favor again? ⁹ Can he have cut off his favor forever? Is the decree of evil complete for all generations? ¹⁰ Can God have forgotten to have pity? Or has he gotten too angry to sustain his compassion forever? ¹¹ And I said, "It is my sickness; they have forgotten the might of the right hand of the Most High." [ANOTHER TARGUM: And I said, "It is my petition, years that he shortened by days."] ¹² I will remember the acts of God, for I will remember your wonders from of old. ¹³ And I meditated on all your good works, and I will speak of the intricacy of your miracles. ¹⁴ O God, because your ways are holy, what God is great like the God of Israel? ¹⁵ You are the God who works wonders; you have made known your might among the peoples. ¹⁶ You have redeemed your people with the strength of your arm, the sons that Jacob sired and whom Joseph fed, forever. ¹⁷ They saw your presence in the midst of the sea, O God; they saw your might by the sea; the Gentiles trembled, even the deeps will be shaken. ¹⁸ The clouds of heaven made water descend, the heights gave voice; also comes the hail, your arrows, and are ablaze. ¹⁹ The sound of your outcry was heard in the sphere; lightning lit up the world, the earth rattled and shook. ²⁰ In the sea of Suph [was] your path, and your highway in the many waters; and the track of your steps were not discerned. ²¹ You guided your people as a flock, by the hand of Moses and Aaron.

Spiritual Awareness

Introduction

This Psalm was composed when the Judeans had settled in Babylon. That land was not their homeland, but it started to feel like home. This would have happened as the next generation who never saw Jerusalem and the Holy Temple was born. During this period, there was a time of spiritual slumber. The Psalmist searches through the chronicles of ancient Israeli history to demonstrate that the LORD saved Israel even in their bleakest moments. The LORD promised that a remnant of the community would always survive.

Superscript

To the Sefirah Netzach, who grants victory. Concerning the providences of God's hand. A psalm of Asaf.

Verse two

The Psalmist speaks about compelling people to activate their latent spiritual and moral energy, which is happier and often remains dormant and neglected deep within us. Even in bad times, one should never forget to offer their prays and praise to the LORD.

In the day of my trouble, I have sought my Master, but my hand melted away into the night without ceasing; therefore, my soul refuses to be comforted.

Verse three

When I wish to reflect on God, I become agitated; if I desire to meditate, my spirit enshrouds itself. Meditate on this verse.

Verse eight

The Psalmist questioned whether the mercy and love of God from the Sefirah Chesed was gone forever.

Is the loving-kindness from the Sefirah Chesed at an end forever? Has He laid down the decree for generation upon generation?

Verse nine

Has God ceased to grant favor and, in anger, shut off His compassion? Meditate upon this verse.

Verse fourteen

In this verse, Israel declares that the LORD is the sole, true, and absolute power over everything.

You are the power, O worker of wonders! You have made known to the nations Your invincible might.

Verse twenty

The destructive impact of the pillar of fire and clouds that preceded the parting of the Sea of Reeds (the Red Sea in most Bibles), accomplished by violent earthshaking and thunderstorms, is remembered. The entire story is not retold. Just saying that the LORD led the flock with Moses and Aaron is enough for the reader to recall the event.

Thus You have led Your people like a flock by the hand of Moses and Aaron.

Psalm 78

New American Standard 1995	Hebrew

Psa. 78:0 A †Maskil of Asaph.

Psa. 78:1 ᵃListen, O my people, to my ¹instruction;
ᵇIncline your ears to the words of my mouth.
2 I will ᵃopen my mouth in a parable;
I will utter ᵇdark sayings of old,
3 Which we have heard and known,
And ᵃour fathers have told us.
4 We will ᵃnot conceal them from their children,
But ᵇtell to the generation to come the praises of the LORD,
And His strength and His ᶜwondrous works that He has done.

Psa. 78:5 For He established a ᵃtestimony in Jacob
And appointed a ᵇlaw in Israel,
Which He ᶜcommanded our fathers
That they should ¹ᵈteach them to their children,
6 ᵃThat the generation to come might know, *even* ᵇthe children *yet* to be born,
That they may arise and ᶜtell *them* to their children,
7 That they should put their confidence in God
And ᵃnot forget the works of God,
But ᵇkeep His commandments,

מַשְׂכִּיל לְאָסָף **Psa. 78:1**

הַאֲזִינָה עַמִּי תּוֹרָתִי הַטּוּ אָזְנְכֶם לְאִמְרֵי־פִי ‎2 ‎:

אֶפְתְּחָה בְמָשָׁל פִּי אַבִּיעָה חִידוֹת מִנִּי־קֶדֶם ‎3 ‎: אֲשֶׁר

שָׁמַעְנוּ וַנֵּדָעֵם וַאֲבוֹתֵינוּ סִפְּרוּ־לָנוּ ‎4 ‎: לֹא נְכַחֵד |

מִבְּנֵיהֶם לְדוֹר אַחֲרוֹן מְסַפְּרִים תְּהִלּוֹת יְהוָה

וֶעֱזוּזוֹ וְנִפְלְאוֹתָיו אֲשֶׁר עָשָׂה ‎5 ‎: וַיָּקֶם עֵדוּת |

בְּיַעֲקֹב וְתוֹרָה שָׂם בְּיִשְׂרָאֵל אֲשֶׁר צִוָּה אֶת־אֲבוֹתֵינוּ

לְהוֹדִיעָם לִבְנֵיהֶם ‎6 ‎: לְמַעַן יֵדְעוּ | דּוֹר אַחֲרוֹן בָּנִים

יִוָּלֵדוּ יָקֻמוּ וִיסַפְּרוּ לִבְנֵיהֶם ‎7 ‎: וְיָשִׂימוּ בֵאלֹהִים

כִּסְלָם וְלֹא יִשְׁכְּחוּ מַעַלְלֵי־אֵל וּמִצְוֹתָיו יִנְצֹרוּ ‎8 ‎: וְלֹא

8 And [a]not be like their fathers,
A [b]stubborn and rebellious generation,
A generation that [c]did not [1]prepare its heart
And whose spirit was not [d]faithful to God.

Psa. 78:9 The sons of Ephraim [1]were [a]archers equipped with bows,
Yet [b]they turned back in the day of battle.

10 They [a]did not keep the covenant of God
And refused to [b]walk in His law;

11 They [a]forgot His deeds
And His [1]miracles that He had shown them.

12 [a]He wrought wonders before their fathers
In the land of Egypt, in the [b]field of Zoan.

13 He [a]divided the sea and caused them to pass through,
And He made the waters stand [b]up like a heap.

14 Then He led them with the cloud by [a]day
And all the night with a [b]light of fire.

15 He [a]split the rocks in the wilderness
And gave *them* abundant drink like the ocean depths.

16 He [a]brought forth streams also from the rock
And caused waters to run down like rivers.

Psa. 78:17 Yet they still continued to sin against Him,

יִהְיוּ ׀ כַּאֲבוֹתָם דּוֹר סוֹרֵר וּמֹרֶה דּוֹר לֹא־הֵכִין לִבּוֹ

9 וְלֹא־נֶאֶמְנָה אֶת־אֵל רוּחוֹ ׃ בְּנֵי־אֶפְרַיִם נוֹשְׁקֵי רוֹמֵי־

10 קָשֶׁת הָפְכוּ בְּיוֹם קְרָב ׃ לֹא שָׁמְרוּ בְּרִית אֱלֹהִים

11 וּבְתוֹרָתוֹ מֵאֲנוּ לָלֶכֶת ׃ וַיִּשְׁכְּחוּ עֲלִילוֹתָיו

12 וְנִפְלְאוֹתָיו אֲשֶׁר הֶרְאָם ׃ נֶגֶד אֲבוֹתָם עָשָׂה פֶלֶא

13 בְּאֶרֶץ מִצְרַיִם שְׂדֵה־צֹעַן ׃ בָּקַע יָם וַיַּעֲבִירֵם וַיַּצֶּב־מַיִם

14 כְּמוֹ־נֵד ׃ וַיַּנְחֵם בֶּעָנָן יוֹמָם וְכָל־הַלַּיְלָה בְּאוֹר

15 אֵשׁ ׃ יְבַקַּע צֻרִים בַּמִּדְבָּר

16 וַיַּשְׁקְ כִּתְהֹמוֹת רַבָּה ׃ וַיּוֹצִא נוֹזְלִים מִסָּלַע וַיּוֹרֶד

17 כַּנְּהָרוֹת מָיִם ׃ וַיּוֹסִיפוּ עוֹד לַחֲטֹא־לוֹ לַמְרוֹת

18 עֶלְיוֹן בַּצִּיָּה ׃ וַיְנַסּוּ־אֵל בִּלְבָבָם לִשְׁאָל־אֹכֶל לְנַפְשָׁם ׃

19 וַיְדַבְּרוּ בֵּאלֹהִים אָמְרוּ הֲיוּכַל אֵל לַעֲרֹךְ

To ^arebel against the Most High in the desert.

18 And in their heart they ^aput God to the test

By asking ^bfood according to their desire.

19 Then they spoke against God;

They said, "^aCan God prepare a table in the wilderness?

20 "Behold, He ^astruck the rock so that waters gushed out,

And streams were overflowing;

Can He give bread also?

Will He provide ^{1b}meat for His people?"

Psa. 78:21 Therefore the LORD heard and ¹was ^afull of wrath;

And a fire was kindled against Jacob

And anger also mounted against Israel,

22 Because they ^adid not believe in God

And did not trust in His salvation.

23 Yet He commanded the clouds above

And ^aopened the doors of heaven;

24 He ^arained down manna upon them to eat

And gave them ^{1b}food from heaven.

25 Man did eat the bread of ¹angels;

He sent them ²food ^{3a}in abundance.

26 He ^acaused the east wind to blow in the heavens

And by His ¹power He directed the south wind.

27 When He rained ¹meat upon them like the dust,

שִׁלַּח בָּמִּדְבָּר: 20 הֵן הִכָּה־
צוּר ׀ וַיָּזוּבוּ מַיִם וּנְחָלִים
יִשְׁטֹפוּ הֲגַם־לֶחֶם יוּכַל תֵּת
אִם־יָכִין שְׁאֵר לְעַמּוֹ: 21 לָכֵן ׀
שָׁמַע יְהוָה וַיִּתְעַבָּר וְאֵשׁ
נִשְּׂקָה בְיַעֲקֹב וְגַם־אַף עָלָה
בְיִשְׂרָאֵל: 22 כִּי לֹא הֶאֱמִינוּ
בֵּאלֹהִים וְלֹא בָטְחוּ
בִּישׁוּעָתוֹ: 23 וַיְצַו שְׁחָקִים
מִמָּעַל וְדַלְתֵי שָׁמַיִם פָּתַח:
24 וַיַּמְטֵר עֲלֵיהֶם מָן לֶאֱכֹל
וּדְגַן־שָׁמַיִם נָתַן לָמוֹ: 25
לֶחֶם אַבִּירִים אָכַל אִישׁ
צֵידָה שָׁלַח לָהֶם לָשֹׂבַע: 26
יַסַּע קָדִים בַּשָּׁמָיִם וַיְנַהֵג
בְּעֻזּוֹ תֵימָן: 27 וַיַּמְטֵר
עֲלֵיהֶם כֶּעָפָר שְׁאֵר וּכְחוֹל
יַמִּים עוֹף כָּנָף: 28 וַיַּפֵּל
בְּקֶרֶב מַחֲנֵהוּ סָבִיב
לְמִשְׁכְּנֹתָיו: 29 וַיֹּאכְלוּ
וַיִּשְׂבְּעוּ מְאֹד וְתַאֲוָתָם יָבִא
לָהֶם: 30 לֹא־זָרוּ מִתַּאֲוָתָם
עוֹד אָכְלָם בְּפִיהֶם: 31 וְאַף

Even [a]winged fowl like the sand of the seas,

28 Then He let *them* fall in the midst of [1]their camp,

Round about their dwellings.

29 So they [a]ate and were well filled,

And their desire He gave to them.

30 [1]Before they had satisfied their desire,

[a]While their food was in their mouths,

31 The [a]anger of God rose against them

And killed [1]some of their [b]stoutest ones,

And [2]subdued the choice men of Israel.

32 In spite of all this they [a]still sinned

And [b]did not believe in His wonderful works.

33 So He brought [a]their days to an end in [1]futility

And their years in sudden terror.

Psa. 78:34 When He killed them, then they [a]sought Him,

And returned and searched [b]diligently for God;

35 And they remembered that God was their [a]rock,

And the Most High God their [b]Redeemer.

36 But they [a]deceived Him with their mouth

And [b]lied to Him with their tongue.

37 For their heart was not [a]steadfast toward Him,

Nor were they faithful in His covenant.

אֱלֹהִים ׀ עָלָה בָהֶם וַיַּהֲרֹג בְּמִשְׁמַנֵּיהֶם וּבַחוּרֵי יִשְׂרָאֵל הִכְרִיעַ: 32 בְּכָל־זֹאת חָטְאוּ־עוֹד וְלֹא־הֶאֱמִינוּ בְּנִפְלְאוֹתָיו: 33 וַיְכַל־בַּהֶבֶל יְמֵיהֶם וּשְׁנוֹתָם בַּבֶּהָלָה: 34 אִם־הֲרָגָם וּדְרָשׁוּהוּ וְשָׁבוּ וְשִׁחֲרוּ־אֵל: 35 וַיִּזְכְּרוּ כִּי־אֱלֹהִים צוּרָם וְאֵל עֶלְיוֹן גֹּאֲלָם: 36 וַיְפַתּוּהוּ בְּפִיהֶם וּבִלְשׁוֹנָם יְכַזְּבוּ־לוֹ: 37 וְלִבָּם לֹא־נָכוֹן עִמּוֹ וְלֹא נֶאֶמְנוּ בִּבְרִיתוֹ: 38 וְהוּא רַחוּם ׀ יְכַפֵּר עָוֹן וְלֹא־יַשְׁחִית וְהִרְבָּה לְהָשִׁיב אַפּוֹ וְלֹא־יָעִיר כָּל־חֲמָתוֹ: 39 וַיִּזְכֹּר כִּי־בָשָׂר הֵמָּה רוּחַ הוֹלֵךְ וְלֹא יָשׁוּב: 40 כַּמָּה יַמְרוּהוּ בַמִּדְבָּר יַעֲצִיבוּהוּ בִּישִׁימוֹן: 41 וַיָּשׁוּבוּ וַיְנַסּוּ אֵל וּקְדוֹשׁ יִשְׂרָאֵל הִתְווּ: 42 לֹא־זָכְרוּ אֶת־יָדוֹ יוֹם אֲשֶׁר־פָּדָם מִנִּי־צָר: 43 אֲשֶׁר־שָׂם בְּמִצְרַיִם

<table>
<tr><td valign="top">

38 But He, being *a*compassionate, [1]*b*forgave *their* iniquity and did not destroy *them;*
And often He [2]*c*restrained His anger
And did not arouse all His wrath.
39 Thus *a*He remembered that they were but *b*flesh,
A [1]*c*wind that passes and does not return.

Psa. 78:40 How often they *a*rebelled against Him in the wilderness
And *b*grieved Him in the *c*desert!
41 Again and again they [1]*a*tempted God,
And pained the *b*Holy One of Israel.
42 They *a*did not remember *b*His [1]power,
The day when He *c*redeemed them from the adversary,
43 When He performed His *a*signs in Egypt
And His *b*marvels in the field of Zoan,
44 And *a*turned their rivers to blood,
And their streams, they could not drink.
45 He sent among them swarms of *a*flies which devoured them,
And *b*frogs which destroyed them.
46 He gave also their crops to the *a*grasshopper
And the product of their labor to the *b*locust.
47 He [1]destroyed their vines with *a*hailstones
And their sycamore trees with frost.

</td><td dir="rtl" valign="top">

אֽוֹתֹתָיו וּמוֹפְתָיו בִּשְׂדֵה־
צֹֽעַן ׃ 44 וַיַּהֲפֹךְ לְדָם יְאֹרֵיהֶם
וְנֹזְלֵיהֶם בַּל־יִשְׁתָּיֽוּן ׃ 45
יְשַׁלַּח בָּהֶם עָרֹב וַיֹּאכְלֵם
וּצְפַרְדֵּעַ וַתַּשְׁחִיתֵם ׃ 46 וַיִּתֵּן
לֶחָסִיל יְבוּלָם וִֽיגִיעָם
לָאַרְבֶּה ׃ 47 יַהֲרֹג בַּבָּרָד
גַּפְנָם וְשִׁקְמוֹתָם בַּֽחֲנָמַל ׃ 48
וַיַּסְגֵּר לַבָּרָד בְּעִירָם
וּמִקְנֵיהֶם לָרְשָׁפִֽים ׃ 49
יְשַׁלַּח־בָּם ׀ חֲרוֹן אַפּוֹ עֶבְרָה
וָזַעַם וְצָרָה מִשְׁלַחַת מַלְאֲכֵי
רָעִים ׃ 50 יְפַלֵּס נָתִיב לְאַפּוֹ
לֹא־חָשַׂךְ מִמָּוֶת נַפְשָׁם
וְחַיָּתָם לַדֶּבֶר הִסְגִּיר ׃ 51 וַיַּךְ
כָּל־בְּכוֹר בְּמִצְרָיִם רֵאשִׁית
אוֹנִים בְּאָהֳלֵי־חָם ׃ 52 וַיַּסַּע
כַּצֹּאן עַמּוֹ וַיְנַהֲגֵם כַּעֵדֶר
בַּמִּדְבָּֽר ׃ 53 וַיַּנְחֵם לָבֶטַח
וְלֹא פָחָדוּ וְאֶת־אוֹיְבֵיהֶם
כִּסָּה הַיָּֽם ׃ 54 וַיְבִיאֵם אֶל־
גְּבוּל קָדְשׁוֹ הַר־זֶה קָנְתָה
יְמִינֽוֹ ׃ 55 וַיְגָרֶשׁ מִפְּנֵיהֶם ׀

</td></tr>
</table>

48 He gave over their *cattle also to the hailstones

And their herds to bolts of lightning.

49 He *sent upon them His burning anger,

Fury and indignation and trouble,

[1]A band of destroying angels.

50 He leveled a path for His anger;

He did not spare their soul from death,

But *gave over their life to the plague,

51 And *smote all the firstborn in Egypt,

The *first *issue* of their virility in the tents of *Ham.

52 But He *led forth His own people like sheep

And guided them in the wilderness *like a flock;

53 He led them *safely, so that they did not fear;

But *the sea engulfed their enemies.

Psa. 78:54 So *He brought them to His holy [1]land,

To this [2]*hill country *which His right hand had gained.

55 He also *drove out the nations before them

And *apportioned them for an inheritance by measurement,

And made the tribes of Israel dwell in their tents.

56 Yet they [1]*tempted and *rebelled against the Most High God

And did not keep His testimonies,

57 But turned back and *acted treacherously like their fathers;

גּוֹיִם וַיַּפִּילֵם בְּחֶבֶל נַחֲלָה

וַיַּשְׁכֵּן בְּאָהֳלֵיהֶם שִׁבְטֵי

יִשְׂרָאֵל : 56 וַיְנַסּוּ וַיַּמְרוּ אֶת־

אֱלֹהִים עֶלְיוֹן וְעֵדוֹתָיו לֹא

שָׁמָרוּ : 57 וַיִּסֹּגוּ וַיִּבְגְּדוּ

כַּאֲבוֹתָם נֶהְפְּכוּ כְּקֶשֶׁת

רְמִיָּה : 58 וַיַּכְעִיסוּהוּ

בְּבָמוֹתָם וּבִפְסִילֵיהֶם

יַקְנִיאוּהוּ : 59 שָׁמַע אֱלֹהִים

וַיִּתְעַבָּר וַיִּמְאַס מְאֹד

בְּיִשְׂרָאֵל : 60 וַיִּטֹּשׁ מִשְׁכַּן

שִׁלוֹ אֹהֶל שִׁכֵּן בָּאָדָם : 61

וַיִּתֵּן לַשְּׁבִי עֻזּוֹ וְתִפְאַרְתּוֹ

בְיַד־צָר : 62 וַיַּסְגֵּר לַחֶרֶב

עַמּוֹ וּבְנַחֲלָתוֹ הִתְעַבָּר : 63

בַּחוּרָיו אָכְלָה־אֵשׁ

וּבְתוּלֹתָיו לֹא הוּלָּלוּ : 64

כֹּהֲנָיו בַּחֶרֶב נָפָלוּ

וְאַלְמְנֹתָיו לֹא תִבְכֶּינָה : 65

וַיִּקַץ כְּיָשֵׁן אֲדֹנָי כְּגִבּוֹר

מִתְרוֹנֵן מִיָּיִן : 66 וַיַּךְ־צָרָיו

אָחוֹר חֶרְפַּת עוֹלָם נָתַן

לָמוֹ : 67 וַיִּמְאַס בְּאֹהֶל יוֹסֵף

They [b]turned aside like a treacherous bow.

58 For they [a]provoked Him with their [b]high places

And [c]aroused His jealousy with their [d]graven images.

59 When God heard, He [1]was filled with [a]wrath

And greatly [b]abhorred Israel;

60 So that He [a]abandoned the [b]dwelling place at Shiloh,

The tent [1]which He had pitched among men,

61 And gave up His [a]strength to captivity

And His glory [b]into the hand of the adversary.

62 He also [a]delivered His people to the sword,

And [1]was filled with wrath at His inheritance.

63 [a]Fire devoured [1]His young men,

And [1]His [b]virgins had no wedding songs.

64 [1]His [a]priests fell by the sword,

And [1]His [b]widows could not weep.

Psa. 78:65 Then the Lord [a]awoke as *if from* sleep,

Like a [b]warrior [1]overcome by wine.

66 He [1a]drove His adversaries backward;

He put on them an everlasting reproach.

67 He also [a]rejected the tent of Joseph,

And did not choose the tribe of Ephraim,

68 But chose the tribe of Judah,

וּבְשֵׁבֶט אֶפְרַיִם לֹא בָחָר ׃ 68

וַיִּבְחַר אֶת־שֵׁבֶט יְהוּדָה

אֶת־הַר צִיּוֹן אֲשֶׁר אָהֵב ׃ 69

וַיִּבֶן כְּמוֹ־רָמִים מִקְדָּשׁוֹ

כְּאֶרֶץ יְסָדָהּ לְעוֹלָם ׃ 70

וַיִּבְחַר בְּדָוִד עַבְדּוֹ וַיִּקָּחֵהוּ

מִמִּכְלְאֹת צֹאן ׃ 71 מֵאַחַר

עָלוֹת הֱבִיאוֹ לִרְעוֹת בְּיַעֲקֹב

עַמּוֹ וּבְיִשְׂרָאֵל נַחֲלָתוֹ ׃ 72

וַיִּרְעֵם כְּתֹם לְבָבוֹ וּבִתְבוּנוֹת

כַּפָּיו יַנְחֵם ׃

Mount *Zion which He loved.
69   And He *built His sanctuary like the heights,
Like the earth which He has founded forever.
70   He also *chose David His servant
And took him from the sheepfolds;
71   From [1]*the care of the [2]ewes *with suckling lambs He brought him
To *shepherd Jacob His people,
And Israel *His inheritance.
72   So he shepherded them according to the *integrity of his heart,
And guided them with his skillful hands.

References

Psalm 78:0
†Possibly, *Contemplative,* or *Didactic,* or *Skillful Psalm*

Psalm 78:1
[1]Or *law, teaching*
[a]Is 51:4
[b]Is 55:3

Psalm 78:2
[a]Ps 49:4; Matt 13:35
[b]Prov 1:6

Psalm 78:3
[a]Ps 44:1

Psalm 78:4
[a]Ex 12:26; Deut 6:7; 11:19; Job 15:18; Ps 145:4; Is 38:19; Joel 1:3
[b]Ex 13:8, 14; Ps 22:30
[c]Job 37:16; Ps 26:7; 71:17

Psalm 78:5
[1]Lit *make them known*
[a]Ps 19:7; 81:5; Is 8:20
[b]Ps 147:19
[c]Deut 6:4-9
[d]Deut 4:9

Psalm 78:6
[a]Ps 102:18
[b]Ps 22:31
[c]Deut 11:19

Psalm 78:7
[a]Deut 4:9; 6:12; 8:14
[b]Deut 4:2; 5:1, 29; 27:1; Josh 22:5

Psalm 78:8
[1]Or *put right*
[a]2 Kin 17:14; 2 Chr 30:7; Ezek 20:18

[b]Ex 32:9; Deut 9:7, 24; 31:27; Judg 2:19; Is 30:9
[c]Job 11:13; Ps 78:37
[d]Ps 51:10

Psalm 78:9
[1]Or *being*
[a]1 Chr 12:2
[b]Judg 20:39; Ps 78:57

Psalm 78:10
[a]Judg 2:20; 1 Kin 11:11; 2 Kin 17:15; 18:12
[b]Ps 119:1; Jer 32:23; 44:10, 23

Psalm 78:11
[1]Or *wonderful works*
[a]Ps 106:13

Psalm 78:12
[a]Ex chs 7-12; Ps 106:22
[b]Num 13:22; Ps 78:43; Is 19:11; 30:4; Ezek 30:14

Psalm 78:13
[a]Ex 14:21; Ps 74:13; 136:13
[b]Ex 15:8; Ps 33:7

Psalm 78:14
[a]Ex 13:21; Ps 105:39
[b]Ex 14:24

Psalm 78:15
[a]Ex 17:6; Num 20:11; Ps 105:41; 114:8; Is 48:21; 1 Cor 10:4

Psalm 78:16
[a]Num 20:8, 10, 11

Psalm 78:17
[a]Deut 9:22; Is 63:10; Heb 3:16

Psalm 78:18
[a]Ex 17:6; Deut 6:16; Ps 78:41, 56; 95:9; 106:14; 1 Cor 10:9
[b]Num 11:4

Psalm 78:19
[a]Ex 16:3; Num 11:4; 20:3; 21:5; Ps 23:5

Psalm 78:20
[1]Lit *flesh*
[a]Num 20:11; Ps 78:15, 16
[b]Num 11:18

Psalm 78:21
[1]Or *became infuriated*
[a]Num 11:1

Psalm 78:22
[a]Deut 1:32; 9:23; Heb 3:18

Psalm 78:23
[a]Gen 7:11; Mal 3:10

Psalm 78:24
[1]Lit *grain*
[a]Ex 16:4
[b]Ps 105:40; John 6:31

Psalm 78:25
[1]Lit *mighty ones*
[2]Or *provision*
[3]Lit *to satiation*
[a]Ex 16:3

Psalm 78:26
[1]Or *strength*
[a]Num 11:31

Psalm 78:27
[1]Lit *flesh*
[a]Ex 16:13; Ps 105:40

Psalm 78:28
[1]Lit *His*

Psalm 78:29
*a*Num 11:19, 20

Psalm 78:30
[1]Lit *They were not estranged from*
*a*Num 11:33

Psalm 78:31
[1]Lit *among their fat ones*
[2]Lit *caused to bow down*
*a*Num 11:33, 34; Job 20:23
*b*Is 10:16

Psalm 78:32
*a*Num chs 14, 16, 17
*b*Num 14:11; Ps 78:11

Psalm 78:33
[1]Lit *vanity, a mere breath*
*a*Num 14:29, 35

Psalm 78:34
*a*Num 21:7; Hos 5:15
*b*Ps 63:1

Psalm 78:35
*a*Deut 32:4
*b*Ex 15:13; Deut 9:26; Ps 74:2; Is 41:14

Psalm 78:36
*a*Ex 24:7, 8; Ezek 33:31
*b*Ex 32:7, 8; Is 57:11

Psalm 78:37
*a*Ps 51:10; 78:8; Acts 8:21

Psalm 78:38
[1]Lit *covered over, atoned for*
[2]Lit *turned away*
*a*Ex 34:6
*b*Num 14:18-20

[c]Is 48:9

Psalm 78:39
[1]Or *breath*
[a]Job 10:9; Ps 103:14
[b]Gen 6:3
[c]Job 7:7, 16; Ps 103:14; James 4:14

Psalm 78:40
[a]Ps 95:8, 9; 106:43; 107:11; Heb 3:16
[b]Ps 95:10; Is 63:10; Eph 4:30
[c]Ps 106:14

Psalm 78:41
[1]Or *put God to the test*
[a]Num 14:22
[b]2 Kin 19:22; Ps 89:18

Psalm 78:42
[1]Lit *hand*
[a]Judg 8:34
[b]Ps 44:3
[c]Ps 106:10

Psalm 78:43
[a]Ps 105:27
[b]Ex 4:21; 7:3

Psalm 78:44
[a]Ex 7:20; Ps 105:29

Psalm 78:45
[a]Ex 8:24; Ps 105:31
[b]Ex 8:6; Ps 105:30

Psalm 78:46
[a]1 Kin 8:37; Ps 105:34
[b]Ex 10:14

Psalm 78:47
[1]Lit *was killing*

*a*Ex 9:23-25; Ps 105:32

Psalm 78:48
*a*Ex 9:19

Psalm 78:49
[1]Lit *A deputation of angels of evil*
*a*Ex 15:7

Psalm 78:50
*a*Ex 12:29, 30

Psalm 78:51
*a*Ex 12:29; Ps 105:36; 135:8; 136:10
*b*Gen 49:3
*c*Ps 105:23, 27; 106:22

Psalm 78:52
*a*Ex 15:22
*b*Ps 77:20

Psalm 78:53
*a*Ex 14:19, 20
*b*Ex 14:27, 28; Ps 106:11

Psalm 78:54
[1]Lit *border, territory*
[2]Or *mountain*
*a*Ex 15:17
*b*Ps 68:16; Is 11:9
*c*Ps 44:3

Psalm 78:55
*a*Josh 11:16-23; Ps 44:2
*b*Josh 13:7; 23:4; Ps 105:11; 135:12

Psalm 78:56
[1]Or *put to the test*
*a*Ps 78:18
*b*Judg 2:11-13; Ps 78:40

Psalm 78:57
[a]Ezek 20:27, 28
[b]Hos 7:16

Psalm 78:58
[a]Deut 4:25; Judg 2:12; 1 Kin 14:9; Is 65:3
[b]Lev 26:30; 1 Kin 3:2; 2 Kin 16:4; Jer 17:3
[c]Deut 32:16, 21; 1 Kin 14:22
[d]Ex 20:4; Lev 26:1; Deut 4:25

Psalm 78:59
[1]Or *became infuriated*
[a]Deut 1:34; 9:19; Ps 106:40
[b]Lev 26:30; Deut 32:19; Amos 6:8

Psalm 78:60
[1]Some ancient versions read *where He dwelt*
[a]1 Sam 4:11; Ps 78:67; Jer 7:12, 14; 26:6
[b]Josh 18:1

Psalm 78:61
[a]Ps 63:2; 132:8
[b]1 Sam 4:17

Psalm 78:62
[1]Or *became infuriated*
[a]Judg 20:21; 1 Sam 4:10

Psalm 78:63
[1]Or *their*
[a]Num 11:1; 21:28; Is 26:11; Jer 48:45
[b]Jer 7:34; 16:9; Lam 2:21

Psalm 78:64
[1]Or *their*
[a]1 Sam 4:17; 22:18
[b]Job 27:15; Ezek 24:23

Psalm 78:65
[1]Or *sobered up from*
[a]Ps 44:23; 73:20

[b]Is 42:13

Psalm 78:66
[1]Lit *smote*
[a]1 Sam 5:6

Psalm 78:67
[a]Ps 78:60

Psalm 78:68
[a]Ps 87:2; 132:13

Psalm 78:69
[a]1 Kin 6:1-38

Psalm 78:70
[a]1 Sam 16:11, 12

Psalm 78:71
[1]Lit *following*
[2]Lit *ewes which gave suck, He...*
[a]2 Sam 7:8; Is 40:11
[b]Gen 33:13
[c]2 Sam 5:2; 1 Chr 11:2; Ps 28:9
[d]1 Sam 10:1

Psalm 78:72
[a]1 Kin 9:4

Targum

Psa. 78:1 A teaching of the holy spirit, composed by Asaph. Hear, O my people, my Torah; incline your ears to the utterances of my mouth. [2] I will open my mouth in a proverb; I will declare riddles from ancient times. [3] Which we have heard and known, and [which] our fathers told to us. [4] We will not hide it from their sons, recounting the psalms of the LORD to a later generation, and his might, and the wonders that he performed. [5] And he established a witness among those of the house of Jacob, and he decreed a Torah among those of the house of Israel, which he commanded our fathers to teach to their sons. [6] So that [another generation, sons still to be born, should know; they will arise and tell it to their children.] [7] And they will place their hope in God, and not forget the works of God, and they will keep his commandments. [8] And they will not be like their fathers, a stubborn and vexing generation, a generation whose heart was not firm with its lord, and its spirit was not faithful to God. [9] While they were living in Egypt, the sons of Ephraim became arrogant; they calculated the appointed time, and erred; they went out thirty years before the appointed time, with weapons of war, and warriors bearing bows. They turned around and were killed on the day of battle. [10] Because they did not keep the covenant of God and refused to walk in his Torah. [11] And the people, the house of Israel, forgot his deeds and his wonders that he showed them. [12] In front of Abraham, Isaac, and Jacob, and the tribes of their ancestors, he performed wonders in the land of Egypt, the field of Tanis. [13] He split the sea with the staff of Moses their leader, and made them to pass through, and he made the water stand up, fastened like a skin bottle. [14] And he guided them with the cloud by day, and all of the night with the light of fire. [15] He split mountains with the staff of Moses their leader in the wilderness; and he gave drink as if from the great deeps. [16] And he brought forth streams of water from the rock, and he made water come down like flowing rivers. [17] But they continued still to sin before him, to provoke anger in the presence of the Most High in the dry wilderness. [18] And they tempted God in their heart, to ask for food for their souls. [19] And they complained in the presence of the LORD; they said, "Is there the ability in the presence of God to set a table in the wilderness?" [20] Behold, he already has smitten a rock, and water gushed out, and streams flowed; is he also able to give bread, or to arrange food for his people? [21] Then it was heard in the presence of God, and he was angry, and fire was made to come up on those of the house of Jacob, and also harsh anger came up on Israel. [22] For they did not believe in God, and did not put their trust in his redemption. [23] And he commanded the skies above and he opened the windows of heaven. [24] And he made descend on them manna to eat, and he gave them the grain of heaven. [25] The sons of men ate food that came down from the abode of angels; he sent them provisions unto satiety. [26] He made the east wind move in the heavens, and guided the south wind by his strength. [27] And he made flesh descend on them like dust, and flying fowl like the sand of the sea. [28] And he made them fall in the midst of his camp, round about its tents. ²⁹ And they ate and were very satisfied; so he brought to them their craving. ³⁰ They did not turn from their craving, still their food was in their mouth – ³¹ And the anger of God went up on them, and he slew some of their champions, and he subdued the young men of Israel. ³² For all this they sinned again, and did not believe in his wonders. ³³ And he ended their days with nothingness, and their years with disaster. ³⁴ Whenever he killed them, they sought him, repenting; and they will repent and pray in the presence of God. ³⁵ And they remembered, for God is their strength, and the Most High God is their redeemer. ³⁶ And they enticed him with their mouth, and they lie to him with their tongue. ³⁷ Because their heart was not faithful to him, and they did not believe in his covenant. ³⁸ But he is merciful, atoning for their sins, and does not destroy them; and he frequently turns from his anger, and he will not hasten all his wrath against them. ³⁹ And he remembers that they are sons of flesh, a breath that goes away and does not return. ⁴⁰ How they would rebel against him in the wilderness! They would cause anger in his presence in a desolate place. ⁴¹ And they turned and tempted God, and brought regret to the Holy One of Israel. ⁴² They did not remember his miracle, and the day that he redeemed them from the oppressor. ⁴³ Who set out his signs in Egypt, and his wonders in the field of Tanis. ⁴⁴ And he turned their canals to blood, and they could not drink from their streams. ⁴⁵ He will incite against them a mass of wild animals, and exterminate them; likewise frogs, and he will slaughter them. ⁴⁶ And he gave and handed over their grain to the grasshopper, and their toil to the locust. ⁴⁷ And he stripped their vines with hail, and their sycamores with locusts. ⁴⁸ And he handed over their cattle to the hail, and their flocks to sparks of fire. ⁴⁹ He will incite against them two hundred and fifty plagues in the harshness of his anger, in wrath, and in hostility, and in woe; which are sent in due time by evil messengers. ⁵⁰ He will travel on the path of his harshness, not keeping their soul from death, and handing over their cattle to the plague. ⁵¹ And he slew all the firstborn in Egypt, the beginning of their sorrow in the tents of Ham. ⁵² And he led his people like a flock, and guided them like a sheep flock in the wilderness. ⁵³ And he settled them securely, and they did not fear; and the sea covered their enemies. ⁵⁴ And he brought them into the territory of the site of the Temple, the same mountain that his right hand created. ⁵⁵ And he drove out the Gentiles before them, and settled them in the lot of his inheritance, and settled the tribes of Israel in their tents. ⁵⁶ But they tempted and provoked in the presence of God Most High, and they did not keep his testimony. ⁵⁷ And they relapsed and did evil like their fathers; they became bent like a bow that shoots arrows. ⁵⁸ And they caused anger in his presence with their libations; and they made him jealous with their idols and images. ⁵⁹ It was heard in the presence of God, and he became angry, and his soul was very disgusted with Israel. ⁶⁰ And he abandoned the tabernacle of Shiloh, the tent where his presence did abide among the sons of men. ⁶¹ And he handed over his Torah to captivity, and his splendor to the hand of the oppressor. ⁶² And he handed over his people to those who slay with the sword, and became angry with his inheritance. ⁶³ The fire consumed his young men, and his young women were not respected. [64] His priests will fall with the killing of the sword, and his widows had no time to weep. [ANOTHER TARGUM: At the time when the Philistines captured the ark of the LORD, the priests of Shiloh, Hophni and Phinehas fell by the sword; and at the time when they informed his wives, they did not weep, for they too died on that same day.] [65] And the LORD woke up like a sleeper, like a man who opens his eyes from wine. [66] And he smote his oppressors on their behinds with hemorrhoids; he gave them eternal disgrace. [67] And he was disgusted with the tabernacle spread over the territory of Joseph; and he took no pleasure in the tribe of Ephraim. [68] But he was pleased with the tribe of Judah, with Mount Zion that he loves. [69] And he built his sanctuary like the horn of the wild ox, fixed like the earth that he founded forever and ever. [70] And he was pleased with David his servant, and took him from the flocks of sheep. [71] And he brought him [away] from [following] after sucklings to rule over Jacob his people, and over Israel his inheritance. [72] And he reigned over them in the perfection of his heart, and he will guide them by the understanding of his hands.

Spiritual Awareness

Introduction

The Psalmist surveys Israel's history from the time of bondage in Egypt until the reign of King David. This is a span of over four hundred years. The history surveyed is not necessarily in chronological order. The events of these years stem from the LORD, who desired that His Holy Torah should be the supreme authority over Israel. The LORD humbled Israel in Egypt so that they would be ready to accept the Torah at Mount Sinai. The LORD settled the people in the Promised Land as an independent nation. David was anointed the King of Israel. During this period, David met several challenges. The powerful tribe of Ephriam challenged David. They were the descendants of Joseph. They were proud that Joshua ben Nun, the conqueror of the Promised Land, was from their tribe. The Tabernacle and the Ark of the Covenant resided in Shiloh for 369 years. Shiloh was located in Ephriam's territory. Yerevan ben Nevat of Ephriam arose to challenge Solomon, leading to the ten tribes leaving the Kingdom.

Verse two

Asaph believed that he solved the riddle of why the LORD allowed certain events to happen to Israel.

I will open my mouth with a parable; I shall solve riddles from antiquity.

The rest of the Psalm is a recount of history.

Psalm 79

New American Standard 1995	Hebrew
Psa. 79:0 A Psalm of Asaph. **Psa. 79:1** O God, the *a*nations have [1]invaded *b*Your inheritance; They have defiled Your *c*holy temple; They have *d*laid Jerusalem in ruins. 2 They have given the *a*dead bodies of Your servants for food to the birds of the heavens, The flesh of Your godly ones to the beasts of the earth. 3 They have poured out their blood like water round about Jerusalem; And there was *a*no one to bury them. 4 We have become a *a*reproach to our neighbors, A scoffing and derision to those around us. 5 *a*How long, O LORD? Will You be angry forever? Will Your *b*jealousy *c*burn like fire? 6 *a*Pour out Your wrath upon the nations which *b*do not know You, And upon the kingdoms which *c*do not call upon Your name. 7 For they have *a*devoured Jacob And *b*laid waste his [1]habitation. **Psa. 79:8** *a*Do not remember [1]the iniquities of *our* forefathers against us; Let Your compassion come quickly to *b*meet us, For we are *c*brought very low.	מִזְמֹ֗ור לְאָ֫סָ֥ף **Psa. 79:1** אֱֽלֹהִ֡ים בָּ֤אוּ גֹויִ֨ם ׀ בְּֽנַחֲלָתֶ֗ךָ טִ֖מְּאוּ אֶת־הֵיכַ֣ל קָדְשֶׁ֑ךָ שָׂ֖מוּ אֶת־יְרוּשָׁלַ֣͏ִם לְעִיִּֽים׃ 2 נָֽתְנ֞וּ אֶת־נִבְלַ֤ת עֲבָדֶ֨יךָ מַֽאֲכָ֗ל לְעֹ֣וף הַשָּׁמָ֑יִם בְּשַׂ֥ר חֲ֝סִידֶ֗יךָ לְחַיְתֹו־אָֽרֶץ׃ 3 שָׁפְכ֬וּ דָמָ֨ם ׀ כַּמַּ֗יִם סְֽבִיבֹ֨ות יְֽרוּשָׁלִָ֗ם וְאֵ֣ין קֹובֵֽר׃ 4 הָיִ֣ינוּ חֶ֭רְפָּה לִשְׁכֵנֵ֑ינוּ לַ֥עַג וָ֝קֶ֗לֶס לִסְבִיבֹותֵֽינוּ׃ 5 עַד־מָ֣ה יְ֭הוָה תֶּאֱנַ֣ף לָנֶ֑צַח תִּבְעַ֥ר כְּמֹו־אֵ֝֗שׁ קִנְאָתֶֽךָ׃ 6 שְׁפֹ֤ךְ חֲמָתְךָ֗ אֶֽל־הַגֹּויִם֮ אֲשֶׁ֪ר לֹֽא־ יְדָ֫ע֥וּךָ וְעַ֥ל מַמְלָכֹ֑ות אֲשֶׁ֥ר בְּ֝שִׁמְךָ֗ לֹ֣א קָרָֽאוּ׃ 7 כִּ֭י אָכַ֣ל אֶֽת־יַעֲקֹ֑ב וְֽאֶת־נָוֵ֥הוּ הֵשַֽׁמּוּ׃ 8 אַֽל־תִּזְכָּר־לָנוּ֮ עֲוֹנֹ֪ת רִאשֹׁ֫נִ֥ים מַ֭הֵר יְקַדְּמ֣וּנוּ רַחֲמֶ֑יךָ כִּ֖י דַלֹּ֣ונוּ מְאֹֽד׃ 9

9 *Help us, O God of our salvation, for the glory of *Your name;

And deliver us and [1c]forgive our sins *for Your name's sake.

10 *Why should the nations say, "Where is their God?"

Let there be known among the nations in our sight,

*Vengeance for the blood of Your servants which has been shed.

11 Let *the groaning of the prisoner come before You;

According to the greatness of Your [1]power preserve [2]those who are *doomed to die.

12 And return to our neighbors *sevenfold *into their bosom

[1]The *reproach with which they have reproached You, O Lord.

13 So we Your people and the *sheep of Your [1]pasture

Will *give thanks to You forever;

To all generations we will *tell of Your praise.

עָזְרֵנוּ ׀ אֱלֹהֵי יִשְׁעֵנוּ עַל־
דְּבַר כְּבוֹד־שְׁמֶךָ וְהַצִּילֵנוּ
וְכַפֵּר עַל־חַטֹּאתֵינוּ לְמַעַן
שְׁמֶךָ: 10 לָמָּה ׀ יֹאמְרוּ
הַגּוֹיִם אַיֵּה אֱלֹהֵיהֶם יִוָּדַע
בַּגֹּיִים [בַּ][גּוֹיִם] לְעֵינֵינוּ
נִקְמַת דַּם־עֲבָדֶיךָ הַשָּׁפוּךְ:
תָּבוֹא לְפָנֶיךָ אֶנְקַת אָסִיר 11
כְּגֹדֶל זְרוֹעֲךָ הוֹתֵר בְּנֵי
תְמוּתָה: 12 וְהָשֵׁב לִשְׁכֵנֵינוּ
שִׁבְעָתַיִם אֶל־חֵיקָם חֶרְפָּתָם
אֲשֶׁר חֵרְפוּךָ אֲדֹנָי: 13
וַאֲנַחְנוּ עַמְּךָ ׀ וְצֹאן
מַרְעִיתֶךָ נוֹדֶה לְּךָ לְעוֹלָם
לְדֹר וָדֹר נְסַפֵּר תְּהִלָּתֶךָ:

References

Psalm 79:1
[1]Lit *come into*
[a]Lam 1:10
[b]Ps 74:2
[c]Ps 74:3, 7
[d]2 Kin 25:9, 10; 2 Chr 36:17-19; Jer 26:18; 52:12-14; Mic 3:12

Psalm 79:2
[a]Deut 28:26; Jer 7:33; 16:4; 19:7; 34:20

Psalm 79:3
[a]Jer 14:16; 16:4

Psalm 79:4
[a]Ps 44:13; 80:6; Dan 9:16

Psalm 79:5
[a]Ps 13:1; 74:1, 9, 10; 85:5; 89:46
[b]Deut 29:20; Ezek 36:5; 38:19
[c]Ps 89:46; Zeph 3:8

Psalm 79:6
[a]Ps 69:24; Jer 10:25; Ezek 21:31; Zeph 3:8
[b]1 Thess 4:5; 2 Thess 1:8
[c]Ps 14:4; 53:4

Psalm 79:7
[1]Lit *pasture*
[a]Ps 53:4
[b]2 Chr 36:19; Jer 39:8

Psalm 79:8
[1]Or our *former iniquities*
[a]Ps 106:6; Is 64:9
[b]Ps 21:3
[c]Deut 28:43; Ps 116:6; 142:6; Is 26:5

Psalm 79:9

[1]Lit *cover over, atone for*
[a]2 Chr 14:11
[b]Ps 31:3
[c]Ps 25:11; 65:3
[d]Jer 14:7

Psalm 79:10
[a]Ps 42:10; 115:2
[b]Ps 94:1, 2

Psalm 79:11
[1]Lit *arm*
[2]Lit *the children of death*
[a]Ps 102:20

Psalm 79:12
[1]Lit *Their*
[a]Gen 4:15; Lev 26:21, 28; Ps 12:6; 119:164; Prov 6:31; 24:16; Is 30:26
[b]Ps 35:13; Is 65:6, 7; Jer 32:18; Luke 6:38
[c]Ps 74:10, 18, 22

Psalm 79:13
[1]Or *pasturing*
[a]Ps 74:1; 95:7; 100:3
[b]Ps 44:8
[c]Ps 89:1; Is 43:21

Targum

Psa. 79:1 A psalm composed by Asaph about the destruction of the Temple. He said in the spirit of prophecy: O God, the Gentiles are entering your inheritance; they have defiled your Temple, they have made Jerusalem a desolation. [2] They have given the bodies of your servants to the birds of heaven for food, the flesh of your pious ones to the wild beasts. [3] They have poured out their blood like water around Jerusalem, and there is none to bury. [4] We have become a disgrace to our neighbors, a subject of scorn and mockery to our surroundings. [5] How long, O LORD, will you be fierce – forever? [How long] will your zeal burn like fire? [6] Pour out your wrath on the Gentiles who have not known you, and on the kingdoms who have not prayed in your name. [7] For they have destroyed the house of Jacob, and made desolate his Sanctuary. [8] Do not remember against us trespasses which were from the beginning; in haste, may your favors go before us, for we have become very destitute. [9] Help us, O God our redemption, because of your glorious name; and redeem us, and atone for our sins, for the sake of your name. [10] Why should the Gentiles say, "Where is their God?" Let the punishment for the blood of your servants that has been spilled be revealed in our sight among the Gentiles. [11] Let the groan of the prisoners come before you like the great strength of your arm; release the children who have been handed over to death. [12] And give back to our neighbors a seven-fold requital for the punishment of their oaths, and the aspersions they cast on you, O LORD. [13] But we are your people, and the sheep of your pasture; we will give thanks in your presence forever; for all generations we will recite your praise.

Spiritual Awareness

Introduction

The Midrash Shocher Tov explains that Assaf had been distressed when the earth swallowed his father Korach (Numbers 16:31-33). He lost all hope that his father would return. He had a vision that the earth would also swallow the gates of the Temple while the rest of the Sanctuary was destroyed. The vision concluded with these gates being raised to their former glory.

Verse six

The Psalmist asks for the wrath of God to be placed upon the nations who do not believe in the LORD and have not proclaimed His name. The name of the LORD, HaShem or Adonai, is the holiest name in the Universe. It is so sacred that it could not be said outside the Holy of Holies in the Temple in Jerusalem. The only time it was said was at 3:00 PM on Yom Kippur by the High Priest, who offered a sacrifice to the LORD on behalf of the people.

Pour out Your wrath toward the nations that know You not and upon the kingdoms that have not proclaimed your name.

Verse seven

Many times in the Hebrew Scriptures, the nation of Israel is referred to as Jacob when they sinned and Israel when they were righteous.

For he has devoured Jacob, and they have laid waste His habitation.

Verse nine

When Israel was taken into Exile in Babylon many of the people had abandoned the LORD. They could not believe that the LORD would allow the Babylonians to capture them and destroy the Temple. Overtime they came to understand that it was their error that caused the problem. The people returned to the LORD and after 70 years the LORD helped them.

Help us, I God of our salvation for the sake of the glory of Your Name; deliver us, spread forgiveness over our errors for Your Name's sake.

Verse thirteen

The Psalmist says that the people are confident of their future which goes hand in hand with the universal worship of God.

But we, Your people and he flock of Your Pasture, we shall render You homage forever; we shall tell Your fame to generation after generation.

Psalm 80

New American Standard 1995	Hebrew

Psa. 80:0   For the choir director; *set to* †El Shoshannim; °Eduth. A Psalm of Asaph.
 	
Psa. 80:1   Oh, give ear, *a*Shepherd of Israel,
  You who lead *b*Joseph like a flock;
  You who *c*are enthroned *above* the cherubim, shine forth!
2   Before *a*Ephraim and Benjamin and Manasseh, *b*stir up Your power
  And come to save us!
3   O God, *a*restore us
  And *b*cause Your face to shine *upon us,* [1]and we will be saved.
 	
Psa. 80:4   O *a*LORD God *of* hosts,
  *b*How long will You [1]be angry with the prayer of Your people?
5   You have fed them with the *a*bread of tears,
  And You have made them to drink tears in [1]large measure.
6   You make us [1]an object of contention *a*to our neighbors,
  And our enemies laugh among themselves.
7   O God *of* hosts, restore us
  And cause Your face to shine *upon us,* [1]and we will be saved.
 	
Psa. 80:8   You removed a *a*vine from Egypt;
	לַמְנַצֵּחַ אֶל־שֹׁשַׁנִּים **Psa. 80:1**
	עֵדוּת לְאָסָף מִזְמוֹר ׃ ²רֹעֵה
	יִשְׂרָאֵל ׀ הַאֲזִינָה נֹהֵג כַּצֹּאן
	יוֹסֵף יֹשֵׁב הַכְּרוּבִים
	הוֹפִיעָה ׃ ³לִפְנֵי אֶפְרַיִם ׀
	וּבִנְיָמִן וּמְנַשֶּׁה עוֹרְרָה אֶת־
	גְּבוּרָתֶךָ וּלְכָה לִישֻׁעָתָה
	לָּנוּ ׃ ⁴אֱלֹהִים הֲשִׁיבֵנוּ וְהָאֵר
	פָּנֶיךָ וְנִוָּשֵׁעָה ׃ ⁵יְהוָה
	אֱלֹהִים צְבָאוֹת עַד־מָתַי
	⁶עָשַׁנְתָּ בִּתְפִלַּת עַמֶּךָ ׃
	הֶאֱכַלְתָּם לֶחֶם דִּמְעָה
	⁷וַתַּשְׁקֵמוֹ בִּדְמָעוֹת שָׁלִישׁ ׃
	תְּשִׂימֵנוּ מָדוֹן לִשְׁכֵנֵינוּ
	⁸וְאֹיְבֵינוּ יִלְעֲגוּ־לָמוֹ ׃
	אֱלֹהִים צְבָאוֹת הֲשִׁיבֵנוּ
	וְהָאֵר פָּנֶיךָ וְנִוָּשֵׁעָה ׃ ⁹גֶּפֶן
	מִמִּצְרַיִם תַּסִּיעַ תְּגָרֵשׁ גּוֹיִם
	וַתִּטָּעֶהָ ׃ ¹⁰פִּנִּיתָ לְפָנֶיהָ

You [b]drove out the [1]nations and [c]planted it.

9 You [a]cleared *the ground* before it,
And it [b]took deep root and filled the land.

10 The mountains were covered with its shadow,
And [1]the cedars of God with its [a]boughs.

11 It was sending out its branches [a]to the sea
And its shoots to the River.

12 Why have You [a]broken down its [1]hedges,
So that all who pass *that* way pick its *fruit*?

13 A boar from the forest [a]eats it away
And whatever moves in the field feeds on it.

Psa. 80:14 O God *of* hosts, [a]turn again now, we beseech You;
[b]Look down from heaven and see, and take care of this vine,

15 Even the [1][a]shoot which Your right hand has planted,
And on the [2]son whom You have [3]strengthened for Yourself.

16 It is [a]burned with fire, it is cut down;
They perish at the [b]rebuke of Your countenance.

17 Let [a]Your hand be upon the man of Your right hand,
Upon the son of man whom You [b]made strong for Yourself.

18 Then we shall not [a]turn back from You;
[b]Revive us, and we will call upon Your name.

וַתַּשְׁרֵשׁ שָׁרָשֶׁיהָ וַתְּמַלֵּא־
אָרֶץ ׃ 11 כָּסּוּ הָרִים צִלָּהּ
וַעֲנָפֶיהָ אַרְזֵי־אֵל ׃ 12 תְּשַׁלַּח
קְצִירֶהָ עַד־יָם וְאֶל־נָהָר
יוֹנְקוֹתֶיהָ ׃ 13 לָמָּה פָּרַצְתָּ
גְדֵרֶיהָ וְאָרוּהָ כָּל־עֹבְרֵי
דָרֶךְ ׃ 14 יְכַרְסְמֶנָּה חֲזִיר
מִיָּעַר וְזִיז שָׂדַי יִרְעֶנָּה ׃ 15
אֱלֹהִים צְבָאוֹת שׁוּב־נָא
הַבֵּט מִשָּׁמַיִם וּרְאֵה וּפְקֹד
גֶּפֶן זֹאת ׃ 16 וְכַנָּה אֲשֶׁר־
נָטְעָה יְמִינֶךָ וְעַל־בֵּן
אִמַּצְתָּה לָּךְ ׃ 17 שְׂרֻפָה בָאֵשׁ
כְּסוּחָה מִגַּעֲרַת פָּנֶיךָ
יֹאבֵדוּ ׃ 18 תְּהִי־יָדְךָ עַל־
אִישׁ יְמִינֶךָ עַל־בֶּן־אָדָם
אִמַּצְתָּ לָּךְ ׃ 19 וְלֹא־נָסוֹג
מִמֶּךָּ תְּחַיֵּנוּ וּבְשִׁמְךָ נִקְרָא ׃
20 יְהוָה אֱלֹהִים צְבָאוֹת
הֲשִׁיבֵנוּ הָאֵר פָּנֶיךָ וְנִוָּשֵׁעָה ׃

[19] O LORD God of hosts, [a]restore us; Cause Your face to shine *upon us,* [1]and we will be saved.	

References

Psalm 80:1
†Possibly, *to the Lilies*
°Lit *A testimony*

Psalm 80:0
*a*Ps 23:1
*b*Ps 77:15; 78:67; Amos 5:15
*c*Ex 25:22; 1 Sam 4:4; 2 Sam 6:2; Ps 99:1

Psalm 80:2
*a*Num 2:18-24
*b*Ps 35:23

Psalm 80:3
¹Or *that we may*
*a*Ps 60:1; 80:7, 19; 85:4; 126:1; Lam 5:21
*b*Num 6:25; Ps 4:6; 31:16

Psalm 80:4
¹Lit *smoke against*
*a*Ps 59:5; 84:8
*b*Ps 79:5; 85:5

Psalm 80:5
¹Lit *a third part of a*
*a*Ps 42:3; 102:9; Is 30:20

Psalm 80:6
¹Lit *a strife to*
*a*Ps 44:13; 79:4

Psalm 80:7
¹Or *that we may*

Psalm 80:8
¹Or *Gentiles*
*a*Ps 80:15; Is 5:1, 2, 7; Jer 2:21; 12:10; Ezek 17:6; 19:10
*b*Josh 13:6; 2 Chr 20:7; Ps 44:2; Acts 7:45
*c*Jer 11:17; 32:41; Ezek 17:23; Amos 9:15

Psalm 80:9
[a]Ex 23:28; Josh 24:12; Is 5:2
[b]Hos 14:5

Psalm 80:10
[1]Or *its boughs are like the cedars of God*
[a]Gen 49:22

Psalm 80:11
[a]Ps 72:8

Psalm 80:12
[1]Or *walls, fences*
[a]Ps 89:40; Is 5:5

Psalm 80:13
[a]Jer 5:6

Psalm 80:14
[a]Ps 90:13
[b]Ps 102:19; Is 63:15

Psalm 80:15
[1]Or *root*
[2]Or figuratively: *branch*
[3]Or *secured*
[a]Ps 80:8

Psalm 80:16
[a]2 Chr 36:19; Ps 74:8; Jer 52:13
[b]Ps 39:11; 76:6

Psalm 80:17
[a]Ps 89:21
[b]Ps 80:15

Psalm 80:18
[a]Is 50:5
[b]Ps 71:20

Psalm 80:19
[1]Or *that we may*
[a]Ps 80:3

Targum

Psa. 80:1 For praise; concerning those who sit in the Sanhedrin who occupy themselves with the testimony of the Torah; composed by Asaph; a psalm. **2** Caretaker of Israel, hear; you who guide the coffin of Joseph like a flock; you whose presence abides between the cherubim, shine forth. **3** Before Ephraim and Benjamin and Manasseh, stir up your mighty power for us; and it is right for you to redeem us. **4** O God, bring us back from our exile, and shine the splendor of your countenance upon us, and we will be redeemed. **5** O LORD God Sabaoth, how long have you not accepted the prayer of your people! **6** You fed them bread soaked in tears, and you made them drink the wine of tears in triple measure. **7** You made us a source of contention for our neighbors, and our enemies will jeer at them. **8** God Sabaoth, bring us back from our exile, and shine the splendor of your countenance upon us, and we will be redeemed. **9** The house of Israel, which is likened to a vine, you brought out of Egypt; you chased away the Gentiles from the land of Israel and planted them. **10** You cleared out the Canaanites before them, and you uprooted their roots and filled the land. **11** The mountains of Jerusalem cover the shadow of the temple, and the academies, say the scholars, are strong, which are likened to mighty cedars. **12** You made branches grow, you sent out her pupils to the Great Sea, and her children to the river Euphrates. **13** Why have you attacked her walls? and [now] all those who pass on the way are pruning her. **14** The boar from the forest will root her up, and the wild cock will be sustained by her. **15** God Sabaoth, turn now, look from heaven, and see, and remember this vine in mercy. **16** And the branch that your right hand planted, and the King Messiah whom you made mighty for yourself. **17** [It is] being burned by fire and crushed; they will perish because of the rebuke that [comes] from your presence. **18** Let your hand be on the man to whom you have sworn with your right hand, on the son of man whom you made mighty for yourself. **19** We will not turn away from the fear of you; you will sustain us and we will call on your name. **20** O LORD God Sabaoth, bring us back from exile; shine the splendor of your countenance upon us and we will be redeemed.

Spiritual Awareness

Introduction

This Psalm was dedicated to the generations of Israelites who lived in Exile in Babylon. From the establishment of the nation of Israel, the people prepared for attacks from the nations surrounding them. The Ten Tribes that constituted the northern kingdom disappeared after the Assyrian invasion. In the Babylonian Exile, the people taken were kept together in Susa and Babylon. This foreign land did become home to future generations. The children born in Babylonia and Susa only knew about the Promised Land and the LORD's Temple through the stories that were passed down by the family and community.

Superscript

The superscript is addressed to the Sefirah Netzach. It is also for roses as a testimony. The rose was a metaphor for Israel. She was weak like rose petals, but Israel's thorns were from the LORD. Thorns protect roses from being destroyed by animals. The thorns are a metaphor for the LORD's protection.

To the Sefirah Netzach who grants victory, for roses; as a testimony, a psalm of Asaf.

Verse one

In this verse, the name Joseph means all the tribes from Jacob. The Psalmist indicates what Joseph's role was in Israel's history. When Joseph was first taken to Egypt, he was tempted to abandon his love for the LORD. He could have engaged in activities that were against the LORD's law. Instead, Joseph demonstrated his beliefs and convictions. Using foresight, it was Joseph being sold into slavery, and the Midianites then sold him to Egypt, which allowed Jacob's family to survive a seven-year famine. Joseph can be viewed as a savior for the people. Therefore, Jews should try to emulate Joseph. They need to stay close to the LORD by following the Laws of the Torah and the words of the Prophets; in other words, they should emulate Joseph. The Psalmist asks for the Light of the LORD to shine upon Israel, thus removing the dark age that the nation was in.

O Shepherd of Israel, incline Your ear! You Who lead Joseph like a flock, O You Who are enthroned upon the Cheribum, shine forth.

Verses four through seven

These verses constitute a cry for help for the people in Babylon's Exile. The people prayed that the Sefirah Gevurah would intervene and bring justice. The people, in general, felt that their exile punishment was too severe for the violations of the Torah committed by the people.

O God, God of Hosts, until when, have You fixed the afterglow of Your wrath to the prayers of Your people?

You have fed them with the bread of tears; You have made them drain their measured drink with tears.

You make us the target of strife for our neighbors; and our enemies mock as they please.

O God of Hosts, lead us back and cause Your countenance to shine so that we shall be saved.

Verses eight through eleven

The usage of the "vine" is an allegory for Israel. Ezekiel portrays Israel as a vine. He explained that the vine was the noblest among all plants because of its fruit. A midrash about Adam and Eve says that the LORD allowed them to take one thing from the Garden of Eden. That item was a vine. Therefore, wine became a sacred drink. The first plant planted by Noah was the vine from the Garden of Eden. In this Psalm the vine is a metaphor for Israel.

"Mountains were covered by its shadow" refers to the branches of the trees that held the fruit harvest.

Israel occupied a central position in the world's trade lanes. The two main trade routes went through Israel. The city of Meggido was at the crossroads of the trading lanes. Therefore, this city was fought over for centuries. The nation that controlled this city had control of taxing the traders who traveled through it.

> **You carry a vine out of Egypt; You drive out nations and plant it.**
> **You cleared a place before it; it took root and filled the land.**
> **Mountains were covered with its shadow, and their branches became cedars of God.**
> **It stretches its fruit – its branches to the sea and its sucking shoots toward the river.**

Verses fifteen and sixteen

Israel is the Son of God because the first group of men to recognize the LORD as 'Father' was Israel. Israel was also known as the intelligent collaborator in the LORD's work of salvation for all humanity.

The foundation which Your right hand has laid, the son whom You have made strong for Yourself.

Burned by fire, cut down, they perished utterly before the threat of Your countenance.

Verse seventeen

"The might of your spirit" this a common expression used for the spirit of the LORD that descends upon a prophet. It is common in Ezekiel (1:3, 3:21, 37:1, 40:1).

May the might of Your spirit come upon the man of Your right hand, upon the son of mankind whom You have made strong for Yourself.

APPENDIX

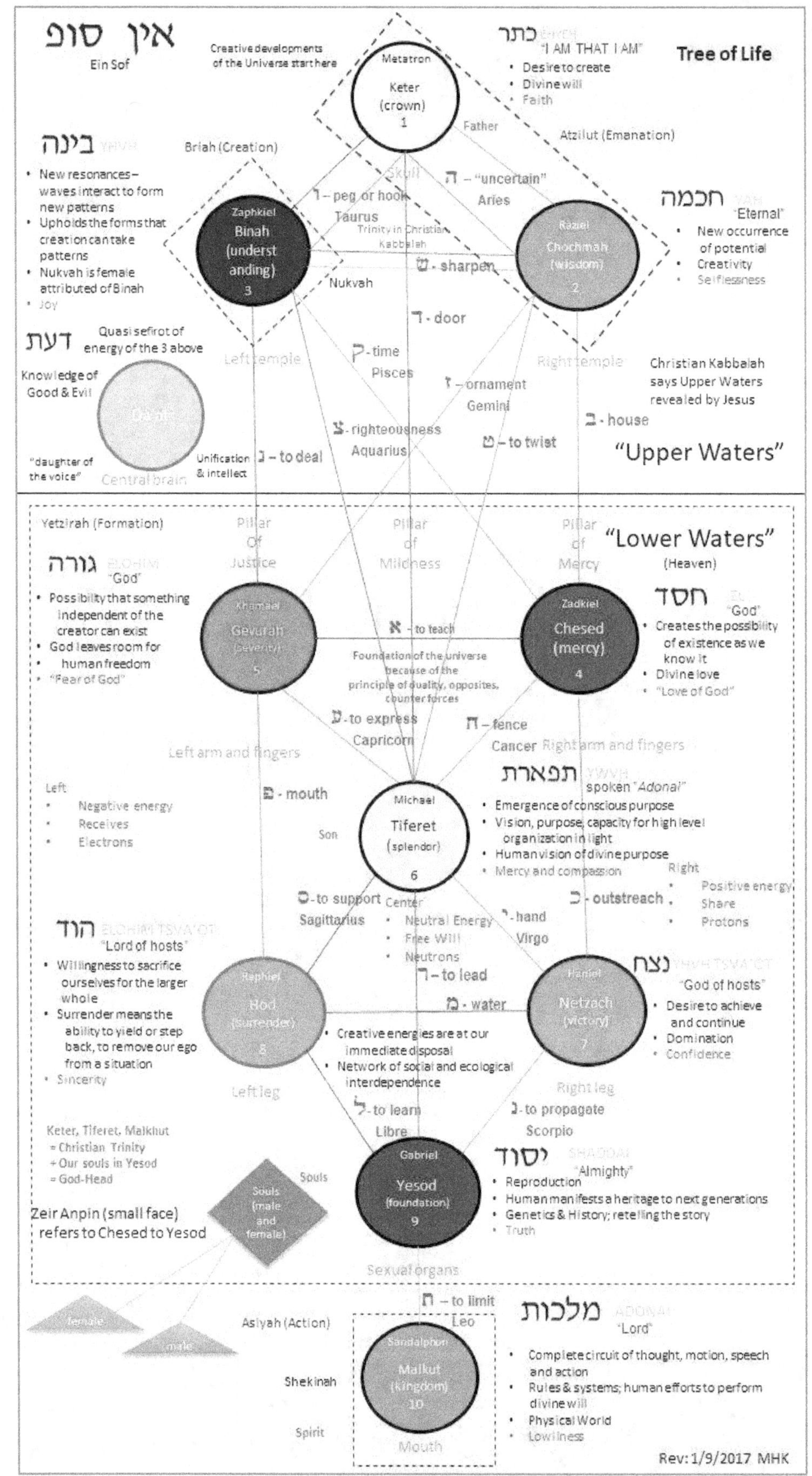

אין סוף
Ein Sof
Tree of Life
Creative developments of the Universe start here
כתר
EHYEH
"I AM THAT I AM"
• Desire to create
• Divine will
• Faith
Metatron
Keter (crown)
1
Father
Skull
Briah (Creation)
Atzilut (Emanation)
בינה
YHVH
ה – "uncertain"
Aries
ו – peg or hook
Taurus
Trinity in Christian Kabbalah
• New resonances – waves interact to form new patterns
• Upholds the forms that creation can take patterns
• Nukvah is female attributed of Binah
• Joy
Zaphkiel
Binah (understanding)
3
ש – sharpen
Nukvah
Raziel
Chochmah (wisdom)
2
חכמה
YAH
"Eternal"
• New occurrence of potential
• Creativity
• Selflessness
דעת
Quasi sefirot of energy of the 3 above
Knowledge of Good & Evil
ד - door
ק - time
Pisces
ז – ornament
Gemini
Christian Kabbalah says Upper Waters revealed by Jesus
ב - house
Daat
Left temple
Right temple
"daughter of the voice"
Unification & intellect
Central brain
צ - righteousness
Aquarius
נ – to deal
מ – to twist
"Upper Waters"
Yetzirah (Formation)
Pillar Of Justice
Pillar of Mildness
Pillar of Mercy
"Lower Waters"
(Heaven)
גורה
ELOHIM
"God"
• Possibility that something independent of the creator can exist
• God leaves room for human freedom
• "Fear of God"
Khamael
Gevurah (severity)
5
א – to teach
Foundation of the universe because of the principle of duality, opposites, counter forces
Zadkiel
Chesed (mercy)
4
חסד
EL
"God"
• Creates the possibility of existence as we know it
• Divine love
• "Love of God"
ע - to express
Capricorn
ח – fence
Cancer
Right arm and fingers
Left arm and fingers
Left
• Negative energy
• Receives
• Electrons
תפארת
YWVH
spoken "Adonai"
• Emergence of conscious purpose
• Vision, purpose, capacity for high level organization in light
• Human vision of divine purpose
• Mercy and compassion
פ - mouth
Michael
Tiferet (splendor)
6
Son
ר - outreach
Right
• Positive energy
• Share
• Protons
הוד
ELOHIM TSVA'OT
"Lord of hosts"
• Willingness to sacrifice ourselves for the larger whole
• Surrender means the ability to yield or step back, to remove our ego from a situation
• Sincerity
ס - to support
Sagittarius
Center
• Neutral Energy
• Free Will
• Neutrons
י - hand
Virgo
ד – to lead
מ - water
Raphiel
Hod (surrender)
8
Haniel
Netzach (victory)
7
נצח
YHVH TSVA'OT
"God of hosts"
• Desire to achieve and continue
• Domination
• Confidence
• Creative energies are at our immediate disposal
• Network of social and ecological interdependence
Left leg
Right leg
Keter, Tiferet, Malkhut
= Christian Trinity
+ Our souls in Yesod
= God-Head
ל – to learn
Libre
ב – to propagate
Scorpio
יסוד
SHADDAI
"Almighty"
Zeir Anpin (small face) refers to Chesed to Yesod
Gabriel
Yesod (foundation)
9
Souls
Souls (male and female)
• Reproduction
• Human manifests a heritage to next generations
• Genetics & History; retelling the story
• Truth
Sexual organs
ת – to limit
Leo
מלכות
ADONAI
"Lord"
female
male
Asiyah (Action)
Sandalphon
Malkut (kingdom)
10
• Complete circuit of thought, motion, speech and action
• Rules & systems; human efforts to perform divine will
• Physical World
• Lowliness
Shekinah
Spirit
Mouth
Rev: 1/9/2017 MHK

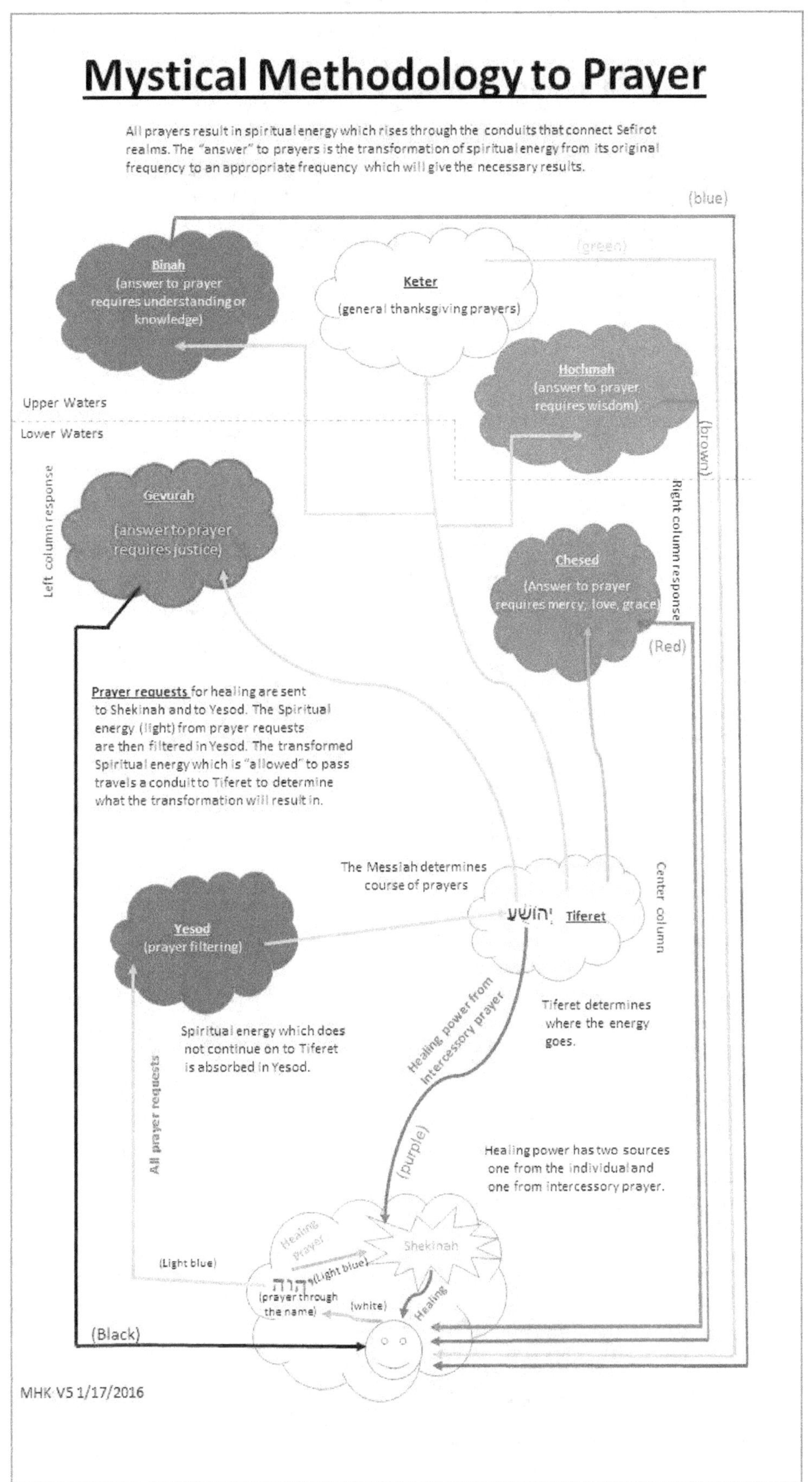

Mystical Methodology to Prayer

All prayers result in spiritual energy which rises through the conduits that connect Sefirot realms. The "answer" to prayers is the transformation of spiritual energy from its original frequency to an appropriate frequency which will give the necessary results.

(blue)
(green)
(brown)
(Red)
(purple)
(Light blue)
(Black)
(white)

Binah
(answer to prayer requires understanding or knowledge)

Keter
(general thanksgiving prayers)

Hochmah
(answer to prayer requires wisdom)

Upper Waters
Lower Waters

Left column response
Right column response
Center column

Gevurah
(answer to prayer requires justice)

Chesed
(Answer to prayer requires mercy, love, grace)

Prayer requests for healing are sent to Shekinah and to Yesod. The Spiritual energy (light) from prayer requests are then filtered in Yesod. The transformed Spiritual energy which is "allowed" to pass travels a conduit to Tiferet to determine what the transformation will result in.

The Messiah determines course of prayers

יהושע Tiferet

Yesod
(prayer filtering)

Tiferet determines where the energy goes.

Spiritual energy which does not continue on to Tiferet is absorbed in Yesod.

Healing power from intercessory prayer

All prayer requests

Healing power has two sources one from the individual and one from intercessory prayer.

Healing Prayer

Shekinah

(light blue)

יהוה
(prayer through the name)

Healing

MHK V5 1/17/2016

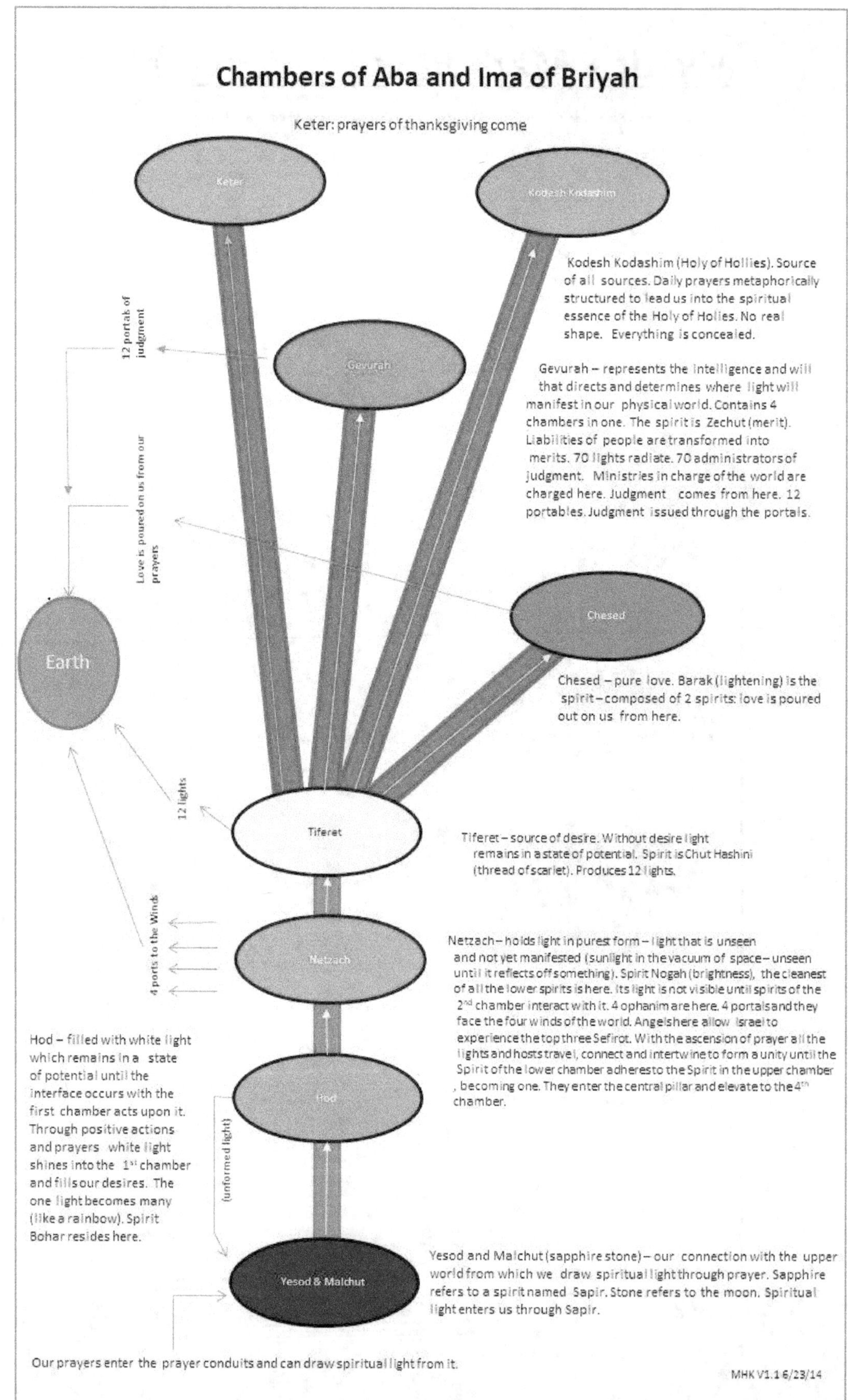

Chambers of Aba and Ima of Briyah
Keter: prayers of thanksgiving come
Keter
Kodesh Kodashim
Gevurah
Chesed
Earth
Tiferet
Netzach
Hod
Yesod & Malchut
12 portals of judgment
Love is poured on us from our prayers
12 lights
4 ports to the Winds
(unformed light)
Kodesh Kodashim (Holy of Hollies). Source of all sources. Daily prayers metaphorically structured to lead us into the spiritual essence of the Holy of Hollies. No real shape. Everything is concealed.
Gevurah – represents the intelligence and will that directs and determines where light will manifest in our physical world. Contains 4 chambers in one. The spirit is Zechut (merit). Liabilities of people are transformed into merits. 70 lights radiate. 70 administrators of judgment. Ministries in charge of the world are charged here. Judgment comes from here. 12 portables. Judgment issued through the portals.
Chesed – pure love. Barak (lightening) is the spirit – composed of 2 spirits: love is poured out on us from here.
Tiferet – source of desire. Without desire light remains in a state of potential. Spirit is Chut Hashini (thread of scarlet). Produces 12 lights.
Netzach – holds light in purest form – light that is unseen and not yet manifested (sunlight in the vacuum of space – unseen until it reflects off something). Spirit Nogah (brightness), the cleanest of all the lower spirits is here. Its light is not visible until spirits of the 2nd chamber interact with it. 4 ophanim are here. 4 portals and they face the four winds of the world. Angels here allow Israel to experience the top three Sefirot. With the ascension of prayer all the lights and hosts travel, connect and intertwine to form a unity until the Spirit of the lower chamber adheres to the Spirit in the upper chamber, becoming one. They enter the central pillar and elevate to the 4th chamber.
Hod – filled with white light which remains in a state of potential until the interface occurs with the first chamber acts upon it. Through positive actions and prayers white light shines into the 1st chamber and fills our desires. The one light becomes many (like a rainbow). Spirit Bohar resides here.
Yesod and Malchut (sapphire stone) – our connection with the upper world from which we draw spiritual light through prayer. Sapphire refers to a spirit named Sapir. Stone refers to the moon. Spiritual light enters us through Sapir.
Our prayers enter the prayer conduits and can draw spiritual light from it.
MHK V1.1 6/23/14

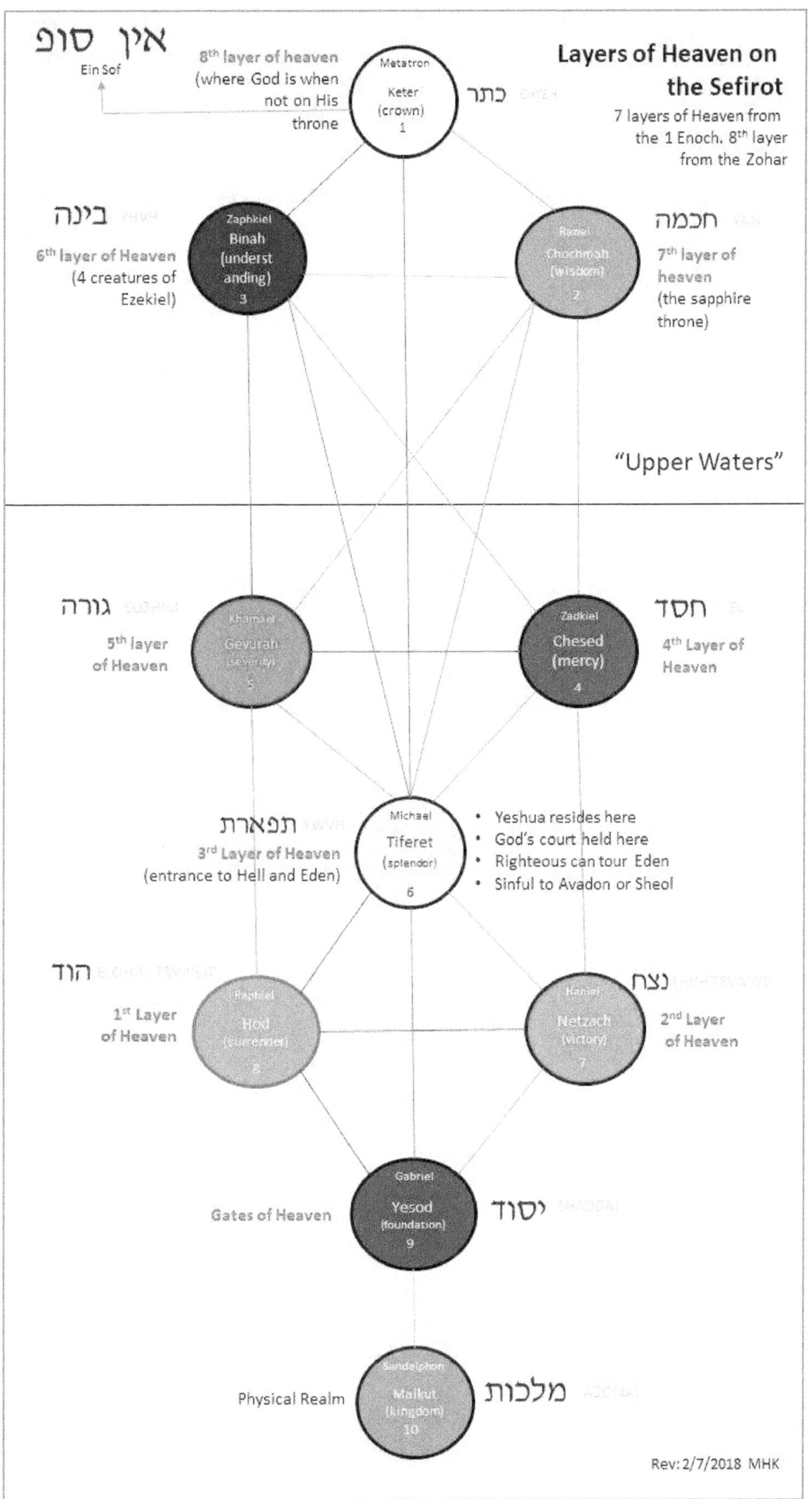

אֵין סוֹף
Ein Sof
Layers of Heaven on the Sefirot
7 layers of Heaven from the 1 Enoch. 8th layer from the Zohar
8th layer of heaven (where God is when not on His throne)
Metatron
Keter (crown)
1
כתר
בינה
6th layer of Heaven (4 creatures of Ezekiel)
Zaphkiel
Binah (understanding)
3
חכמה
7th layer of heaven (the sapphire throne)
Raziel
Chochmah (wisdom)
2
"Upper Waters"
גורה
5th layer of Heaven
Khamael
Gevurah (severity)
5
חסד
4th Layer of Heaven
Zadkiel
Chesed (mercy)
4
תפארת
3rd Layer of Heaven (entrance to Hell and Eden)
Michael
Tiferet (splendor)
6
• Yeshua resides here
• God's court held here
• Righteous can tour Eden
• Sinful to Avadon or Sheol
הוד
1st Layer of Heaven
Raphael
Hod (surrender)
8
נצח
2nd Layer of Heaven
Haniel
Netzach (victory)
7
Gates of Heaven
Gabriel
Yesod (foundation)
9
יסוד
Physical Realm
Sandalphon
Malkut (kingdom)
10
מלכות
Rev: 2/7/2018 MHK

Michael Harvey Koplitz